A Concise History of
Posters: 1870–1970

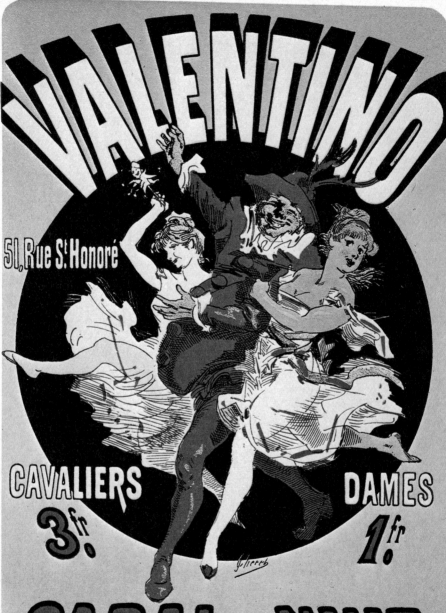

A Concise History of

Posters:
1870–1970

by John Barnicoat

HARRY N. ABRAMS, INC. *Publishers* NEW YORK

To Allie with love

★1   (Frontispiece) JULES CHÉRET *Bal Valentino* 1869

★For additional information
  see List of Illustrations (pp. 266–75)

Contents

CHAPTER ONE

Art Posters

THE FIRST POSTERS

Art is man's creation, yet words and pictures are also the form of his language. If art is not primarily communication but creation, then posters, with their prescribed function of advertising and propaganda, would seem to be only a secondary art form. Yet posters, in the first hundred years of their existence, have also had a curious relationship with painting. Besides translating the visual art movements of the twentieth century into consumer media, the nature and limitations of advertising have sometimes influenced the form and direction of painting. The first occasion when the poster had such an effect was at its coming of age in 1870.

In 1866 Jules Chéret (1836–1933) started to produce colour lithographic posters from his own press in Paris. *Bal Valentino* (1869) is an example. The form of the poster as we know it dates from this time because of the coincidence of two factors: certain technical improvements in lithographic printing and the presence of Chéret himself.

The process of lithography was not new; it had been invented in 1798 by Alois Senefelder in Austria, although his methods were not perfected until later. By 1848 it was possible to print sheets at the rate of 10,000 an hour. In 1858 Chéret produced his first colour lithograph design, *Orphée aux Enfers*. His real contribution to the history of the poster, however, began when he returned to Paris after a seven-year stay in England and started to produce posters from the new English machinery based on Senefelder's designs. Chéret drew his designs straight onto the lithographic stone – re-establishing lithography as a direct creative medium, as Goya and others had used it at the beginning of the century. For some years since then, lithography had often been used merely as a means of reproducing other art. In spite of this, a tradition of lithographed

1

7

◄ *2 JULES CHÉRET *La Pantomime* 1891

book illustration existed in France, and technically one can trace the poster's evolution through the printed page.

Gavarni, pseudonym of Guillaume Chevalier (1804–66), was an illustrator for the periodical *Charivari* and specialized in everyday themes. Denis Auguste Raffet (1804–60) had designed two advertisements for Norvin's *History of Napoleon* which were really part of his illustrations for this work. Tony Johannot (1803–52) designed an advertisement, *Don Quichotte* (1845), which was one of the eight hundred illustrations that he had made for the famous novel. Although these works and others like them were advertisements consisting of words and pictures, their connection with the printed book is too close for them to be considered posters, and their small size made it difficult to distinguish them among other advertising material on public display.

Though public announcements themselves have a long history and their roots have been traced back to antiquity, it is more realistic to start the development of this form of communication with an example such as the earliest printed advertisement in England, by William Caxton in 1477. In seventeenth-century France there was a ban against posting bills without permission. Sign-boards in France in 1761 were fixed flat against walls for safety by order of Louis XV – thus anticipating the hoarding, or billboard. As early as 1715 one finds a picture advertisement for folding umbrellas, and in 1800 *Bonne Bierre de Mars*, an illustration of young couples drinking at an inn – both from France. But these two examples were no larger than a book page. It is only in 1869, when Chéret's posters were first appearing, that one of those small advertisements seems to show some indication of new, simple patterns of design that were later to become the essence of poster technique. This was a design by Manet:
3 *Champfleury – Les Chats* – a composition easily retained by the memory, since it is made up of flat shapes.

This form of simple visual pattern-making was not so apparent in Chéret's work, which, at a hundred years' distance, seems based on the traditional compositions associated with European mural painting. It is legitimate to compare the design of Chéret's posters with the murals and the tall, upright, rectangular compositions of Tiepolo.

8

J. ROTHSCHILD, ÉDITEUR, 43, RUE St-ANDRÉ-DES-ARTS, PARIS

CHAMPFLEURY

LES CHATS

HISTOIRE – MŒURS – ANECDOTES

ILLUSTRÉ   ILLUSTRÉ

PAR   PAR

E. Delacroix   Ed. Manet

Breughel   Ok'Saï

Viollet-le-Duc   Mind, Ribot

UN VOLUME ORNÉ DE NOMBREUSES GRAVURES

PRIX : 5 FRANCS

Paris. — Typ. Gillet, rue du Jubilné. I.

5   HENRI DE TOULOUSE-LAUTREC *Divan Japonais* 1893

◀ 4   JULES CHÉRET *Carnaval 1894: Théâtre de l'Opéra* 1893

Chéret studied at the Beaux-Arts in Paris while still working as a lithographer's apprentice and, in addition to Tiepolo's work, one can detect in his draughtsmanship a similarity with drawings by Fragonard and Watteau. In an interview with the English critic Charles Hiatt, Chéret even maintained that for him posters were not necessarily a good form for advertising but that they made excellent murals.

This is the reason Chéret has become known as the first name in posters. It is not that his designs are masterpieces of the art of advertising, but that his posters, over a thousand of them, are magnificent works of art. Instead of re-interpreting the great murals of the past for the public of his day by creating large salon canvases, he found a new place for his work – the street.

Part of Paris had recently been re-designed by Baron Haussmann, the architect of Napoleon III's new capital. Many of the old and well-loved buildings of the days of the Revolution had been pulled down, and in their place a city of great style, although perhaps of monotonous regularity, was being constructed. The wide boulevards and intersections have been admired by city planners ever since. They were, at the time of their construction, also a practical solution to the problems of mob-control by artillery. On the austere walls of this new city, Chéret's posters appeared as a new vital art form. Writers like Joris-Karl Huysmans and Edmond de Goncourt, as well as countless critics and art-historians of the time, have drawn attention to the explosion of colour created by Chéret.

It is because of the material success of this public display of fine art that posters became known as the art gallery of the street. In the case of Chéret's works, this phrase is a just description. However, the idea that one has merely to display paintings in the road to provide high-class art for the masses is a basic error that well-intentioned publicists have often failed to understand. Chéret had taken the technique of the lithograph book-illustrator, but had used the scale and style of a master like Tiepolo. However, the real contribution of his genius lay in his introduction of a third element to these two familiar sources – one that was to give his undoubted ability as a traditional draughtsman the currency of popular language.

2
6

*6 GIOVANNI TIEPOLO *St Tecla praying for the plague-stricken* 1759 ▶

Reine de Joie
par
Victor Joze
chez tous les libraires

Imp. Edw. ANCOURT & Cie. PARIS

8 THOMAS THEODOR HEINE *Simplicissimus* 1897

◀ ★7 HENRI DE TOULOUSE-LAUTREC *Reine de Joie* 1892

9　Bartholomew Fair, London 1721. Traditional signs and displays anticipate the billboard

Chéret took the visual language of popular folk art used to decorate circus programmes – such as the one for Le Cirque Rancy in the middle 1860s – and enlarged this, as he was able to do with his experience as a trained lithographer. His posters bring together a traditional technique and an appreciation of great mural art, but also that essential ingredient – the feel of the popular idiom. In their

16　programme covers and ephemera, the circuses and fairgrounds of England and France had for many years used designs that were striking and alive. The large fairground-booth paintings, such as those

9　in use at Bartholomew Fair in England, and the big American

advertisements for circuses from the United States on tour in England during Chéret's stay there, would also have contributed to his ideas. The American works were printed in small sections using wood blocks. All these elements may be said to have contributed to the appearance of the poster, but it was without doubt the effort of this one man that gave the poster its special character.

In *Bal Valentino*, Chéret established the dynamic quality of his work. The dancing figure of a clown with two girls seems to spring out at one, and this effect is accentuated by the lettering which fans outwards, the top word 'Valentino' being in suggested 3-D. In this

10 WILHELM LISZT *Ver Sacrum Kalender* 1903

11   LUDWIG VON ZUMBUSCH Cover for *Jugend* (No. 40) 1897

case the lettering is part of the design, but in Chéret's work as a whole the lettering was added later (by a friend, Madaré, who died in 1894), which reinforces the fact that he was primarily a mural painter and not an advertising man. But *Bal Valentino* is an awkward design compared with some of his later posters, for example,

4   *Théâtre de l'Opéra* (1894) or *Pippermint* (1899). In these works the whole effect is lighter and freer.

Chéret created a type of girl who soon represented a popular concept for the 1880s and '90s in the same way that others – Roger Vadim, for example, in the 1950s – have done for later generations. His favourite model was a Danish actress and dancer, Charlotte Wiehe. She appears in Chéret's posters as irrepressibly happy, dancing, laughing and irresponsible. She was popularly called 'La Chérette', and girls imitated her looks. To catch sight of the posters is to be caught up in an extrovert release of happiness – a pictorial equivalent of the expectation aroused by the sound of the cork released from a bottle of champagne. The flowing, effervescent and transparent glazes of Chéret's posters were perhaps inspired by the colours of the butterfly wings that he kept by him as he worked. Layers of delicate tints are arranged carefully and simply with minimum technical fuss to produce an effect of spontaneity that makes many mass-culture productions seem laboured by comparison.

Today we probably find Chéret's work more representative of the end of a great European tradition than the start of new developments; the link with Tiepolo is more obvious to us than it would perhaps have been to his contemporaries. At that time, the innovations in his work would have seemed more startling. In his early work the striking use of black as a colour and the interlocking flat shapes provided a break with traditional interpretation of solid form and illusion of depth, which younger artists, such as Toulouse-Lautrec and Bonnard were to develop even further. Henry van de Velde, one of the great spokesmen for Art Nouveau, mentioned Chéret as an important source for that decorative art movement. One can see this connection

12   in a poster such as *Les Girard* (1879), with the restless character of the composition and the long pointed elements in the design.

12 JULES CHÉRET *Les Girard* 1879

13   ALPHONSE MUCHA *Papier Job* 1897

14 ALPHONSE MUCHA *Gismonda* 1894   15 VICTOR SCHUFINSKY *Lucifer Girl* 1904

In addition to his influence on Art Nouveau, Chéret's work had a significant effect on Seurat. Two of Seurat's paintings, *Le Chahut* (1889–91) and *Le Cirque* (1890–91), illustrate the use of circus backgrounds or dancers rather than that dependence on nature characteristic of Impressionist naturalism of the '70s. *Le Cirque*, in fact, echoes elements found in Chéret's *Spectacle-Promenade de l'Horloge* of a decade earlier. Seurat's art, in any case, had formalized the natural world, but Chéret had also provided an artificial concept which Seurat found useful. Seurat himself made a design in the poster manner – a cover for the novel *L'Homme à Femmes* (1889) – which owes a great deal to Chéret's *L'Amant des Danseuses* (1888).

Chéret's influence grew as younger artists found that the poster, through its very nature, was to develop a form of visual shorthand in which ideas could be expressed simply and directly. His posters remain for all time the first steps in this direction. They exactly convey the spirit of the era known as *fin de siècle*, but lift it into an illusory world of almost allegorical style – a decorative comment on the social life of the streets where the posters appeared.

Henri de Toulouse-Lautrec (1864–1901), by contrast, accentuated the style of Chéret's work, but used it to describe what went on inside the lives of the inhabitants of those streets. Whereas pupils of Chéret, such as Georges Meunier, in a poster such as *L'Elysée Montmartre* (1895), and Lucien Lefèvre in *Electricine* (1895), illustrated the cabarets of Montmartre or domestic scenes in Chéret's manner, Lautrec's contribution to the developing style of the poster went further than this. He dramatized his own personal experience and used the medium of the poster as a means of expression: thus the
5 poster *Divan Japonais* (1893) is his portrait of a friend, Jane Avril. The element of caricature, humorous and satirical, the simple, flat shapes and the decorative line, were all devices that Lautrec could employ in a poster but which he could not express so simply and directly within the conventions of the painting of his time. His posters have a quality of broad silhouette less apparent in his paintings and drawings of the same subjects, and this simplified statement is one that re-appears in the work of many painters during the first half of the twentieth century. Lautrec owes much of his style to the example of

*16   ANONYMOUS Cover for circus programme *c.* 1864

Chéret, who, in turn, had spoken of him as *un maître*. Lautrec's posters, however, are a significant extension of Chéret's achievement. Chéret relates the poster to the art of the past while establishing it as a form. Lautrec was to relate the poster to future developments in painting while consolidating that form.

Chéret designed the poster advertising the opening of the Moulin Rouge in 1889: Lautrec was commissioned to make one for the same establishment in 1891 featuring their new star La Gouloue. The change in style from the world of Tiepolo to the modern scene is obvious. Lautrec seems to have eliminated the traditional elements in Chéret's work while exaggerating certain aspects of broad pattern-making latent there. Lautrec's design takes the poster further away from the book illustration or the traditional easel painting.

His work was not necessarily popular. His lithograph *Mlle Marcelle Lender*, which he dedicated to the German periodical *Pan*, caused the resignation of its publishers when they attempted to print the work. Lautrec's exhibition in London, at the Goupil Galleries in 1898, was a failure. Even Yvette Guilbert – the star of the show at the Divan Japonais (who appears with her head out of the picture in the poster that is obviously dedicated to a member of her audience, Jane Avril) – felt that the album designed for her by Lautrec was too hideous to publish. Edmond de Goncourt complained of what one can only translate as a 'sick' interpretation of women by the new modern artists. However, the English art critic, Charles Hiatt, correctly understood the element of caricature, comparing Lautrec's designs with the work of Hogarth and Rowlandson. There is a sharp contrast between the posters of Chéret, aimed to please and delight, and those of Lautrec which appeared to be 'ugly' and were uncomfortable. Hiatt describes them as half-attractive and half-repelling.

Lautrec's posters – he made only thirty-one during his short life of thirty-seven years (1864–1901) – are a major contribution to the history of posters. It is a strange thought that, had he lived as long as Chéret (a remarkable ninety-seven years), he would have died only in 1961. Lautrec's contribution to the twentieth century was indirectly reflected in all poster design, for he helped to establish the direct quality of the poster as an art form. But no poster artist of his calibre followed him in France - the impact of his work affected painting, for example, through the work of Pablo Picasso.

In *The Blue Room* of 1901, Picasso gives us a portrait of his own room shared with models and friends; hanging on the wall is Lautrec's poster, *May Milton* (1895). It was in 1900 that Picasso first arrived in Paris, but French *fin-de-siècle* design was available to him earlier, in Barcelona, in the form of reproductions in magazines like *Le Rire*, *La Vie Parisienne*, *Gil Blas* and *L'Assiette au Beurre*. In Barcelona, the Catalan tavern, El Quatre Gats (The Four Cats), was modelled on the Paris cabaret, Le Chat Noir – later presided over by Aristide Bruant, himself a subject of one of Lautrec's best-known posters. Picasso designed for this tavern a poster in the style of the

17 RAMON CASAS *Anís del Mono*
1898

Arts and Crafts movement in England. One of the leading personalities of the Barcelona circle was the Spanish painter, Ramon 17
Casas. Aside from his poster, *Anís del Mono* (the monkey was the
trade mark of this group), he made another called *Pulchinel-Lis 4
Gats*: both of these have echoes in Picasso's later work, such as the
Acrobat's Family with an Ape (1905). These links with early poster
design, and ultimately with Lautrec's broad caricature, seem to
have a direct continuation in the simple, monumental forms that
appear in Picasso's paintings, even as late as the 1930s.

Another artist whose posters may have contributed to the shift
from naturalism towards narrative or descriptive journalism was the

19 Swiss, Théophile Alexandre Steinlen, who arrived in Paris in 1881 – the year Picasso was born. Both Steinlen and Lautrec continued to explore the area of social commentary in the visual arts, an aspect already studied by artists like Daumier. Some of Steinlen's posters are direct social comment: *Mothu et Doria* (1894) shows two smokers, one gloved, in his top hat and cape, offering a light to the cigarette stub of the other, dressed in a cap, wearing a red scarf, hand in pocket. The same descriptive observation appears in Steinlen's poster *La Rue* (1896). Others are of domestic scenes with children and cats, which remind one of the Blue Period of Picasso's work. Steinlen had also contributed a famous series of designs to the original rooms of Le Chat Noir. The effect of all these posters on one of the great artists of the twentieth century during his youth has never been assessed, yet the change towards simple description and decoration in much twentieth-century painting from the elaborate naturalism of the nineteenth owes something to the new freedom conferred by the popular idiom of the poster.

18 HENRI DE TOULOUSE-LAUTREC *Jane Avril* 1893

*19   THÉOPHILE-ALEXANDRE STEINLEN *La Traite Blanches* 1899

The most characteristic modern style of the turn of the century was Art Nouveau. This movement in the arts, fine and applied, included poster design. As a style, Art Nouveau gave a decorative and ornamental value to linear patterns that were often derived from organic shapes. The term 'Art Nouveau' was applied to the movement in Britain and in the United States; in Germany 'Jugendstil'; in France 'Le style moderne'; in Austria 'Secession'; in Italy 'Stile Liberty'; in Spain 'Modernista'. In each case the interpretation of the style was linked with the idea of the 'new'. It represented, in decorative terms, new social developments, new technology and new expressions of the spirit. For example, in the hands of an artist like Charles Rennie Mackintosh of Glasgow, its patterns seemed to derive from Celtic illuminated manuscripts while at the same time anticipating, particularly in his architecture and furniture design, the styles of the twentieth century.

The style, which grew partly from the English Arts and Crafts movement, was developed by individual countries in Europe and in the United States. In Germany, the special characteristics of Art Nouveau were introduced through the enthusiasm of groups of designers and writers such as those who were responsible for magazines like *Die Jugend*, which was started in 1896. The term 'Jugendstil' was adopted from the name of this journal. Its subtitle – 'Munich's Weekly Magazine of Life and the Arts' – shows that the intention of the 'new' was to integrate art with society. Fritz Dannenberg's poster of a girl astride a giant champagne bottle was made for the journal. Something of the same spirited involvement was also shown in Victor Schufinsky's *Lucifer Girl*. The special characteristic of Jugendstil in poster design is the quality of fantasy, which was usually presented in organic terms and which was also closely related to illustration.

The spirit of the 'new' prompted groups to break away from the academic and to form Secessionist associations, such as those in Munich and Vienna. In Munich, the artists von Stuck, Habermann and Eckmann were involved. In addition to *Die Jugend*, another

40

11

15

29

publication, *Simplicissimus*, appeared in 1896 in Munich and the two journals provided a stimulating incentive for designers, especially in the field of posters. *Simplicissimus* was more satirical than its contemporary and contained a variety of elements, including popular stories, scandals and political cartoons. The posters and illustrations for this magazine by Thomas Theodor Heine (1867-1948) are *8, 194* particularly inventive. Bruno Paul was another contributor, and *20* Leo Putz (1869–1940) made posters in which he used his skill as a draughtsman to create designs that probably appealed as pin-ups.

10 In Vienna, the Secessionists' work was collected together in a remarkable series called *Ver Sacrum* (Rite of Spring). In the various issues of this 'journal' that appeared between 1898 and 1903, there *22* are examples of the work of Klimt, Moser, Hoffmann, Olbrich, *23* Roller and many others. Their designs and the posters they made are more delicate than the sometimes 'heavy' quality of Jugendstil, and there is often a characteristic balance and order that distinguish the work from the asymmetry of Art Nouveau generally. There is a real connection, in style, between this work and the designs made by *21* Mackintosh and his associates at the Glasgow School of Art. Klimt

20   LEO PUTZ
Moderne Galerie
c. 1914

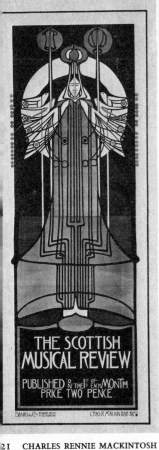

21   CHARLES RENNIE MACKINTOSH
The Scottish Musical Review
1896

22   KOLOMAN MOSER
Ver Sacrum
1903

23   ALFRED ROLLER
Poster for XIVth Exhibition,
Vienna Secession 1902

and others were aware of their work, and the Four of Glasgow
showed at the Eighth Secessionist Exhibition at Munich in 1900.
They also 'stole' the show in Turin in 1902.

In Berlin the founding of the magazine *Pan* by Julius Meier-
Graefe and Otto Bierbaum in 1895 was given striking visual form
by the cover designed by Josef Sattler (1867–1931). Other poster
designers in Berlin included Paul Scheurich, Edmund Edel, Hans
Rudi Erdt, Lucian Bernhard, Julius Klinger, Julius Gipkens, Jupp,
Wiertz and Joseph Steiner. Many of these artists were still dominating
the scene in the 1920s. Some of the posters designed in Austria and

51

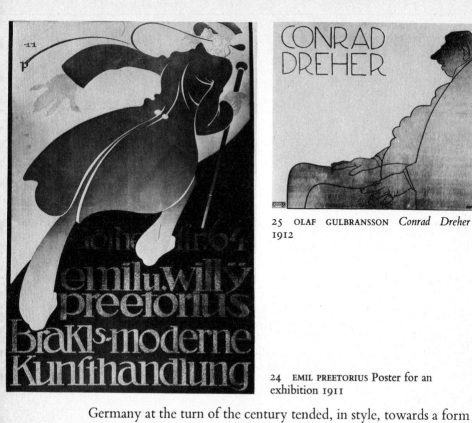

25 OLAF GULBRANSSON *Conrad Dreher* 1912

24 EMIL PREETORIUS Poster for an exhibition 1911

Germany at the turn of the century tended, in style, towards a form of Expressionist realism, while retaining a strong link with the decorative motifs of Jugendstil. Examples taken from the enormous output of remarkable posters are those by Johann Cissarz, Hans Unger (*Estey-Orgein*, 1896), Nikolaus Gysis and Peter Behrens – also associated with Munich – whose designs include *Allgemeine Elektrizitätsgesellschaft* (1910) and his famous *Der Kuss* (1898). Posters designed by Olaf Gulbransson (1873–1958) and Emil Preetorius (b. 1883) carried many of the characteristics of Jugendstil into the post-war world of the twenties. After 1900 the floral decorations as a dominant motif gave way to a more abstract design. The Wiener Werkstätten, which existed from 1903 until 1932, displayed a continued development of this style of work; and the Deutscher Werkbund, founded in 1907 (Gustav Klimt was a founder member), led, after the First World War, to the establishment of the Bauhaus, which became a focal point for formal abstract design.

32

In Germany the motif of flowing shapes, as illustrated so well in the cover by von Zumbusch for *Jugend* No. 40 (1897), becomes linked through the heavy shapes and bright colours of Kandinsky's poster, *Ausstellung Phalanx München* (1901), with the design ideas of the Blaue Reiter group, which came to be recognized as a force in 1911, and which are therefore seen to derive from Munich Jugendstil.

The most famous examples of posters in the 'style moderne' in France were, of course, the work of Toulouse-Lautrec. However, it is known that he had admired the poster *France-Champagne* (1891) by Bonnard, and it was Bonnard who introduced him to the process of lithography. Bonnard made only a few posters, yet a work like *La Revue Blanche* (1894) demonstrates his gift for unusual composition and the subtle sense of humour that he continued to use in his drawings and paintings until his death in 1947. Something of the character of *La Revue Blanche* remained with his work always.

11

27

26

★26 PIERRE BONNARD
La Revue Blanche 1894

27 PIERRE BONNARD *France–Champagne* 1891

28 EUGÈNE GRASSET *Salon des Cent* 1894

Among the most significant elements of Art Nouveau design, particularly in Paris, were the shapes derived from the Japanese print. Some of these designs had appeared on the wrapping paper of articles from the Far East. The famous prints of artists such as Hiroshige, Hokusai and Utamaro belonged to the Ukiyo-e 'School' – work that described the daily life of the street. The subject-matter also included a series of erotic prints. As well as being a direct influence on the European poster, the Japanese print, with its reflection of daily life as well as more glamorous material, has had a profound effect on pictorial advertising. Most posters connected with the Art Nouveau style show a marked similarity of composition which was the European version of the 'Japanese'.

Art Nouveau, which, as we have seen, contained elements of design that anticipated future developments (for example, the furniture of Josef Hoffmann), also included references to the distant past: William Morris's painted furniture and the spirit of medievalism were essential elements among the many factors included in an overworked title that expressed so many transitional styles and manifestations in the arts of 1900. Eugène Grasset expressed

35

in France the same love of the medieval decorators that the Pre-
28 Raphaelites showed in England. Grasset's pupil, Paul Berthon,
wrote of his work:

> You see, our new art is only, and must only be, the continuation
> and development of our art of France choked by the Renaissance.
> What we want is to create an original art without any model but
> nature, without any rule but imagination and logic, using at the
> same time the French flora and fauna as details and following very
> closely the principles which made the medieval arts so thoroughly
> decorative. . . . I myself only try to copy nature in its very essence.
> If I want to see a plant as decoration I am not going to reproduce
> all its nerves as leaves, or the exact tint of its flowers. I may have
> to give the stem of the flowers more harmonious as well as
> geometrical line, or unconventional colours which have never
> been seen in the model I have before me. For instance I shall never
> be afraid to paint my figures with green, yellow or red hair, if these
> tones are to be wanted in the composition of the design.

This significant deviation from naturalism is characteristic of much
Art Nouveau design – although Grasset claimed to dislike Art
Nouveau. It also shows that the considerable licence that was
taken for granted in applied arts, like stained glass or posters, could
also be applied to painting itself.

One of the significant features of the general amalgamation of
styles and media at the turn of the century was that one art form
could and did affect the development of others. The poster, soon
after its coming of age, was able to take part in this exchange. Thus
one of the most characteristic examples of Art Nouveau in any
13 medium is the astonishing poster work of Alphonse Mucha. Mucha
was born in 1860 in the then kingdom of Bohemia, and came to
Paris in 1890. His work went through a phase of Art Nouveau
expression, during which he designed posters in the fashionable
'Byzantine' style of ornamentation, as well as interiors – for example,
for the jeweller, Georges Fouquet – and projects for giant exhibition
buildings. He later left Paris in order to live for a short time in
New York and finally changed the style of his work to become a

36

29 ALPHONSE MUCHA
Salon des Cent 1896

painter of Slavic themes on the grand scale. He died in Prague in
1930. His long working life therefore runs parallel to that of Chéret,
who had also abandoned his fame as a poster designer in order to
become a painter – but of less consequence. (In Chéret's case, failing
eyesight after 1910 probably contributed to his change of working
methods.)

Mucha's best-known posters are those associated with Sarah
Bernhardt, although one feels that her spirit haunts all his poster   29
designs. She was responsible for commissioning him to make his first
successful poster – *Gismonda* (1894), which made his name in Paris.   14
As a painter of the Bernhardt myth, Mucha proved to be her perfect
counterpart. His appreciation of exotic clothes and jewellery found
a living reality in her personality. He accompanied her to New York
and his work was introduced to another world. It is significant that
his designs were so extreme that when Art Nouveau, as a style,
suffered an eclipse and disappeared temporarily from popular favour
during the twenties, Mucha also was forgotten. He was considered

37

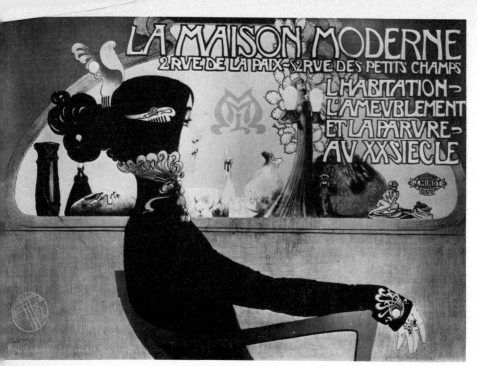

30 MANUEL ORAZI *La Maison Moderne c.* 1905

too local a phenomenon even to find a mention in a history of posters
written by McKnight Kauffer in 1924. This is also an indication of
the uncompromising nature of his considerable contribution to Art
Nouveau: it has even been suggested that the oriental horseshoe-
shaped motifs of Guimard's famous Métro entrances in Paris were,
in fact, derived from the same design found in Mucha's posters.
Until about 1897 his posters were probably executed by his own
hand directly on the stone, but after that date one can detect a less
brilliant manner: much of his work was being done by assistants
because of the great demands made on him. It is interesting to know
that he sometimes worked from photographs, not only for reference
to the complicated draperies but also for the pose of the model.

Other poster makers in France whose work reflected the fashion-
47 able Art Nouveau style included Manuel Orazi (working between
1880 and 1905), who created jewellery for Meier-Graefe's famous

38

shop, which became a centre of design: his poster for *La Maison Moderne* (*c*. 1905) has a wonderful feeling for the fashion accessories of the period. An earlier poster by Maurice Biais (1900) also shows the articles in the shop, which had been founded in 1899 and which rivalled the Maison de l'Art Nouveau. It was the latter, owned by Samuel Bing, from which the name of the movement was derived. Georges de Feure (1868–1928) made a number of designs in the applied arts for Bing and also designed the poster for the fifth exhibition of the Salon des Cent. Many artists made posters for these exhibitions, which were shown at 31 Rue Bonaparte, sponsored by Léon Deschamps; they could be mixed shows or the work of one artist (the total number of exhibits was not allowed to exceed a hundred). De Feure's posters feature fashionable women with pale, sad faces; one of his most elegant was that made for *Le Journal des Ventes* in 1897. Hector Guimard (1867–1942), the architect, also made a poster design, *Exposition Salon du Figaro le Castel Béranger* (1900), in which his well-known designs are related to lettering.

31   HECTOR GUIMARD *Exposition Salon du Figaro le Castel Béranger* 1900

32 EMILE BERCHMANS
Libotte-Thiriar beers *c.* 1897

61   In Belgium, Henri Meunier, Victor Mignot and Privat-Livemont (whose work reflects Mucha's style) were the most important artists to compare with those working in Paris at the end of the nineteenth century. In Liège, the publisher August Benard commissioned 32 Armand Rassenfosse, Emile Berchmans and August Donnay to make designs for him in the late 1880s. Other poster designers in Belgium of importance were Adolphe Crespin, who designed 152 *Alcazar Royal* (1894) with Édouard Duyck, and Henri Evenpoel. On the whole it can be said that many of the designs are more literal and less stylized than other works in this era of the art poster, the work of the Liège school being direct and simple. However, the effects of Paris designs are evident in Berchmans' *Amer Mauguin* or Rassenfosse's *Huile Russe.* In the Netherlands, the work of Braaken-siek shows an affinity with that of Chéret; and two of the leading 202 Dutch poster designers in this period were J.G. Van Caspel and Willy Sluiter. The unusual imagery produced by two Belgian artists, Van de Velde and Felicien Rops, and the Dutch painter Jan Toorop, are discussed below in an examination of the symbolism and iconography of Art Nouveau.

40

In Hungary, Benczur and Rippl-Ronai were contemporaries of Chéret and, as in France, a tradition of advertising for circus performances and other events goes back to the seventeenth and eighteenth centuries. The most famous of the *fin-de-siècle* designers was Arpad Basch, who had trained in Paris, but whose style was still that of the illustrator: he was a particularly fine draughtsman. His work was reviewed in the magazine *The Poster* and an example of his designs was included in *Les Maîtres de l'Affiche*, a monthly series of lithographed posters in reduced size, edited by Roger-Marx and issued in Paris from 1896 to 1900.

33

In Italy, poster design owed a great deal of its technical background to the publishing firm of Ricordi, which had provided the basis for commissioning posters. Among artists who worked for Ricordi were Leopoldo Metlicovitz, Mataloni (*Caffaro Zeitung*, 1900) and Adolfo Hohenstein, whose poster *Tosca* (1899) is a fine example of *fin-de-siècle* art, with its mixture of Art Nouveau decoration and theatrical drama. His posters, *Iris* (1898) and *Esposizione di Elettricità* (1899), also have monumental character. Leonardo Bistlofi's *Prima Esposizione Internazionale d'arte moderna decorativa Torino* (1902) has a Jugendstil quality about it. One of the best-known artists was Leonetto Cappiello (1875–1942). Like many poster designers who

46

33 ARPAD BASCH Poster for Kühnee agricultural machinery *c.* 1900

were working in Paris, he came from elsewhere – in his case, from Italy. He started to make his name in Paris in 1900 and his posters were among the first to anticipate a more modern approach to poster design. Many of them derive from Chéret and other pioneers, but 204 his work also represented a simplified version of *fin-de-siècle* designs which gave them the character of impoverished versions of the older works. In fact, he was the first to appreciate the quickening pace of life in the streets and his posters are a link between the more leisurely world of the end of the nineteenth century and the new era created by the speeding motorist.

In the 1890s the poster boom was at its height. Special editions were made for collectors; posters were sometimes stolen from their position on the walls. There were exhibitions of posters in Paris, and in 1890 a show at the Grolier Club in New York. Ernest Maindron, who had written the first article on posters in 1884 (in Paris) and the first volume on the poster's history in 1886, added a second volume (1886–95) in 1896. The following year a companion volume by various contributors was also issued dealing with posters in other countries. In England, the first volume of *The Studio* contained an article on poster-collecting (Art Nouveau was sometimes known as the 'Studio style') and in 1898 the magazine *The Poster* was founded. The craze for poster-collecting was a short one among the general public, although posters have always been sought after by specialists. Significantly *The Poster* was merged with *The Art Collector* in 1900, reflecting a general decline in the exceptional enthusiasm that the appearance of the poster had originally generated.

In the United States, poster design in the Art Nouveau style was brilliantly shown in the work of Will Bradley (1868–1962). He made 48 a number of designs for *The Chap Book*, to which Toulouse-Lautrec and Aubrey Beardsley had also contributed. After a long and distinguished working life in graphics in the United States, he was awarded the gold medal of the American Institute of Graphic Arts in 1954. Edward Penfield (1886–1926) also produced a number of posters which, like Bradley's, not only used the Paris style but added a clear-cut element that gave a feeling of solidarity to the European designs. Other poster artists in the United States at this

42

34 EDWARD PENFIELD
Design for *Harper's*
(March) 1894

35 WILL CARQUEVILLE
Lippincott's

time were Ethel Reed, Frank Hazenplug and Will Carqueville, all   *35*
of whom worked in the Art Nouveau style. Apart from the effect of
seeing Mucha's work during Sarah Bernhardt's tours, Americans
would have seen magazines and copies of *The Yellow Book*, and the
work of such artists as Grasset, who designed a cover for *Harper's*   *28*
Magazine in 1889 and posters for *The Century*. A first-hand account of
the poster situation comes from the Englishman F. Scotson-Clark,
who visited the United States in the nineties:

> Until the winter of 1894, the artistic poster was practically
> unknown in the United States. The only things of the kind, and
> they were very excellent and very original, were the *Harper's*
> *Magazine* window bills by Edward Penfield. But during the   *34*
> latter part of 1893 and the early half of 1894, the name and work

43

36 Posters in a London street 1899

of Aubrey Beardsley had become known, and popular as was his success amongst a large class in England, his fame was tenfold in America. Every twopenny-halfpenny town had its 'Beardsley Artist', and large cities simply teemed with them. Some borrowed his ideas and adapted them to their own uses; others imitated, until one asked oneself: 'is this done by the English or American B?'

The 'American B' was of course Bradley; and besides Scotson-Clark himself, another English-born artist was at work there – Louis Rhead, who produced some very colourful posters in the Art Nouveau manner. In England, however, the position of Art Nouveau was a strange one. Whereas the style had derived much of its original stimulus from English sources, like the Pre-Raphaelites and William Morris, the application of their ideas as international Art Nouveau was slow to return (the position in neighbouring

37   DUDLEY HARDY *A Gaiety Girl c.* 1895

Scotland was different). James Pryde, who had studied in Paris before returning to England and a subsequent career as a well-known painter gives an account of the difference between the attitude towards poster design in Paris and in London:

> At that time posters in England were, with two or three exceptions, anything but striking, although there were some very interesting poster artists working in Paris. For example, Chéret, who did some notable work for the Divan Japonais, and Toulouse Lautrec, who in addition to affiches for the same café chantant did some remarkable designs for Yvette Guilbert, Jane Avril, Caudieux and others.
>
> Poster art in England was just being redeemed by Dudley Hardy whose *Yellow Girl* for the Gaiety Theatre was a clever piece of work; Maurice Greiffenhagen, later a Royal Academician, who did a poster for the *Pall Mall Budget* and Frederick Walker

5

45

*38   AUBREY BEARDSLEY Poster for Avenue
Theatre, London 1894

39   FRED WALKER *The Woman in White* 1871

39   whose *Woman in White* [1871] really seemed like an enlarged reproduction of a black-and-white drawing of his own.
There was also Aubrey Beardsley's poster for what was then
38   regarded as the advanced theatre in London, the Avenue [1894].
This last found little favour with *Punch* which, referring to it,
made the suggestion: 'ave a new poster. There were oases in the
desert of others designed by regular workers for various firms.
This was the condition of affairs when I decided to become a
poster artist.

Pryde goes on to say that he and his colleague, William Nicholson,
who had also studied in Paris, tackled the problem together. They
did this, in what must then have seemed a very amateurish way, by

46

making paper cut-outs and pasting them onto board. No lettering was included; their intention was that any suitable title could be added later. The fact remains that, in spite of what appears to be an unassuming way of working, they produced original and unorthodox results. They called themselves the Beggarstaff Brothers after seeing the name on a sack ('it seemed such a good hearty old English name') and they admitted designing posters 'to afford the luxury of painting pictures'. The ten or so works they made are all exceptional. *Girl on a Sofa* (1895) was rejected at the time but has 50 now taken its place as one of the outstanding designs of the period in any country. Their work belongs, in style, more to the English Arts and Crafts movement than to international Art Nouveau. It does, however, relate to the posters of Toulouse-Lautrec and one can see their ideas continuing in the work of the great German poster designer, Ludwig Hohlwein; they were pioneers in the use of large flat areas of colour and compositions of extreme simplicity.

Other designers in England at the time, such as Dudley Hardy and 37 John Hassall, produced posters for entertainments in the popular 233 idiom. Although the subject-matter was similar to that of their contemporaries in Paris, they used the cartoonist's imagery and 220 their work suffers, for example, in comparison with Lautrec's. They nevertheless produced some brilliant examples of popular humour.

Posters that were more in the style of Art Nouveau came from Sidney Ransom (working under the pseudonym of Mosnar Yendis) – e.g., his cover for the first volume of *The Poster* in 1899. Walter Crane's posters, which are good examples of Art Nouveau, were too close to his illustrative work, and in any case he expressed an aversion to the element of 'shouting' that posters represented.

The most significant contribution to Art Nouveau posters from England came from Aubrey Beardsley in spite of the close connection between his posters and his illustrative material. The sensitive and the intense are two aspects of art often greeted with suspicion – certainly by the hearty element that existed in Edwardian England. Comic opera and parody were areas of expression in which the English public could treat, with confidence, art that proved too stylized or which made them feel self-conscious. A thoroughgoing aesthete was expected to conform to the abnormal: Beardsley's work was sufficiently uncompromising and he remains one of the most important influences in the history of design. His work provides a link with a new element that was making another contribution to the arts in general and to posters in particular.

POSTERS AND SYMBOLISM

The Symbolist movement, which in France is associated with painters such as Gauguin and Maurice Denis, used some of the devices and decoration of the wider style known as Art Nouveau but in a special way. Briefly, one can say that Symbolist art affected poster design by reintroducing iconography as a pictorial element. Symbolist artists used the writhing linear patterns and amorphous shapes of Art Nouveau to describe things sacred and profane. To the nineteenth century, with its veneers of propriety, it was possible to say something of those areas of human experience that were generally left to the imagination, Images that could express, in equivalent terms, passion and excitement were loaded with classical or religious references, for a society that could thus mask its feelings. Salome, the Sphinx, Pan, Medusa, the child-woman, the serpent, are all subject objects of painting, poster and poetry. Josef Sattler's design 51 for *Pan* (1895) is an example.

One must also remember that at this time the art-collecting public – in England, to take one country as an example – was changing. In place of the Establishment, whose tastes were on the whole conservative and therefore still linked to Classicism and the eighteenth century, we now find a new middle class that had none of these preconceived attachments. At this time, too, the Tractarians, closely associated with the Pre-Raphaelites, were trying to revive a sense of spirituality in the doctrine and liturgy of the Church of England, then one of the central pillars of society. This 'High Church' Movement, Pre-Raphaelitism and the Gothic Revival formed a direct chain of new thinking in religious and artistic terms in England. The effect on architecture as well as poster design is significant. On the Continent, the same process existed and was given expression by writers like Huysmans, who were fascinated by the liturgical rituals of the Catholic Church. He and other artists extended their experiences into more experimental spheres of the occult: black magic, theosophy, the theories of the Rosicrucians and the activities of Sar Joséphin Peladan, whose teachings equated the role of the artist with that of the priest.

The pictorial designs of the artists connected with these movements affect the poster directly because, as documents, their posters and paintings contained pictorial information that did not necessarily have to be presented in a naturalistic way. Enlarged, almost expressionist-like faces, decorative borders composed of eyes, Rosicrucian and ancient signs, are mixed together with little regard for the traditional rules of pictorial composition. Many of the paintings of the Symbolists look like posters, with their allegorical subject-matter, subjective colour and striking imagery. This revival of iconography was of great importance to both painting and graphics. The use of symbols in a design gives that work its own reality, its own unity; objects do not need to be arranged in the naturalistic limits of a single viewpoint that are imposed by a tradition of illusionist easel painting. 43

Most of the leading Symbolist painters also produced posters. Maurice Denis wrote of posters in 1920: 'The important thing is to find a silhouette that is expressive, a symbol which, simply by its forms and colours, can force its attention on a crowd and dominate the passer-by. The post is a banner, an emblem, a sign: *in hoc signo vinces.*'

His remark, made after the initial event, applies to the growing powers of the poster at the turn of the century. Perhaps the most impressive example of commercial symbolism – showing how the advertisement could make use of these developments – is the poster *Delftsche Slaolie* (1895) by the Dutch artist, Jan Toorop. This work contains a mixture of Art Nouveau devices and stylization, as well as a straightforward bottle of salad oil. A brief account of Toorop's background gives an idea of the associations between the various Symbolist groups in Belgium, France and England. He was born in Java in 1858 of Norwegian and Oriental parents. He came to Europe

40   CARL STRAHTMANN Music sheet design, an example of Jugendstil composition

LE JOURNAL DES VENTES.

N⁰ 15 ⁰ᵗ

PARAISSANT LES DIMANCHES

DIRECTION,

CH. VOS ET C⁰

123 RUE DE LA PUTTERIE

BRUXELLES

de Feure

IMP. LEMERCIER, PARIS.

at an early age and in 1882 met Van de Velde, Ensor and Khnopff in Brussels. A poster made by Khnopff in 1891 gives a list of invitées 42 to the 8th exhibition of Les XX, and includes the names of Gauguin, Chéret, Seurat, Crane and Wilson Steer. Toorop also exhibited with Les XX. In addition, his work appeared at the first Salon of the Rose + Croix (1892) in Paris. (Among those who were connected with the Rosicrucian sect and designed posters for the move- 43 ment were Edmond Aman-Jean, Marcel Lenoir, Armand Point, 45 Léonard Sarluis, and Carlos Schwabe.) Toorop was also interested in the work of Beardsley and William Morris; he passed through a phase of socialism, finally becoming a Catholic convert. He died in 1928.

His contemporaries included Félicien Rops (1833–98), who also showed with Les XX. Rops designed only three posters – that for 44 *Les Légendes Flamandes* shows the melodramatic element of the macabre side of his work. Rops was also well known for his erotic drawings and engravings. The element of voyeurism that runs

52

42 FERNAND KHNOPFF *Les XX* 1891

43 ANONYMOUS (possibly by MARCEL LENOIR) *Mérodak* (Salon de la Rose + Croix) *c.* 1897

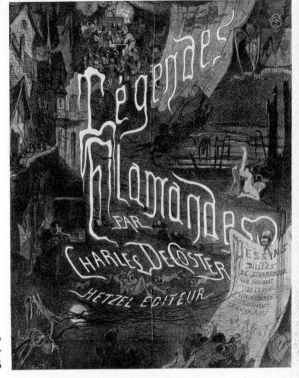

44 FÉLICIEN ROPS *Les Légendes Flamandes* 1858

45 ARMAND POINT and LÉONARD SARLUIS *Salon de la Rose + Croix* 1896

46 ADOLPHO HOHENSTEIN *Iris* 1898

*47 MANUEL ORAZI *Loie Fuller* 1900

THE CHAP BOOK

THANKS GIVING NO.

8 WILL BRADLEY *The Chap Book* 1894

through his work has since become acceptable in public advertising. However, the moralizing element so obvious in Rops's work is absent from the antics displayed in the underwear posters eighty years later – and also from the posters and graphics of the Underground Movement. As a precursor of the freer imagery of the 1960s Rops's work shows that, in spite of a change of attitude, the devices of presenting the semi-naked have remained constant.

The name of Van de Velde is associated with many of the significant developments in the applied arts of the early twentieth century. He was one of the founders of the Deutscher Werkbund in 1907, although as a Belgian he decided to leave Germany in 1914. He recommended as his successor Walter Gropius, who later became the first director of the Bauhaus. Van de Velde died in 1957. He designed only one poster – for the firm of food manufacturers, 55 Tropon (1897) – although he also made a series of related designs for them. This single poster remains a key example of Art Nouveau design in any medium. It shows admirably how a poster could contribute to design, and how, in fact it anticipated some of the developments in decorative abstract painting later on.

The Symbolists made another contribution to the development of pictorial design which affected the course of painting as well as that of design in advertising: they displayed different aspects of the same idea within the same work of art. In this way past and present, and different aspects of the same theme, such as the 'sacred' and the 'profane', could be displayed simultaneously. Furthermore, they combined art forms so that the same idea could exist pictorially, musically and in words. A musical and liturgical event seems to be an apt description for the Solemn Mass at Saint Germain l'Auxerrois on 10 March 1892: music by the superhuman Wagner and a figure who was to become part of *avant-garde* circles in the early twentieth century – Erik Satie. Posters of the Rose + Croix display the same multifarious character and showed the spirit of the nineteenth century in terms of another age. The graphic use of these methods has become part of the language of posters ever since. It was not until the 1960s, however, that another generation was to discover 54 just how meaningful these works had been.

56

*49 JOSEF RUDOLPH WITZEL *Jugend c.* 1900

HIPPY POSTERS

In November 1965 an exhibition of 'Jugendstil and Expressionism
in German Posters' was held at the University Art Gallery on the
Berkeley campus of the University of California. This proved to be
of special interest to designers of a new development in artistic style
– the Hippy poster – a bizarre, stimulating form of decoration that
owes a great deal to Art Nouveau and Symbolist designs of the turn
of the century. There are many points of similarity. In the first place,
designers of the Hippy posters make full use of the past, as though
it were a direct part of their experience; stylistically the past partici-
pates in the present. A poster design such as that in the 1960s by
Robert McClay (*Funky Features*) is related to Rose+Croix designs.
In the 1890s Peladan and his followers were disillusioned with a
world of materialism that proved to be hollow; his search for
spiritual qualities was revived by a section of society in the 1960s.
The long robes, flowing beards, drugs and unisex are expressions of

49

53

57

Brothers Beggarstaff

Plakat

1   JOSEF SATTLER *Pan* 1895

50   BEGGARSTAFF BROTHERS *Girl on a Sofa* 1895

52 BOB MASSÉ Poster for Kitsilano Theatre,
Vancouver 1968

53 ROBERT McCLAY *Funky Features* 1968

both Symbolist and Hippy. The cult of the bizarre has returned with
renewed force in a materialistic society that has multiplied its
52 technical tricks a thousand times but is still no wiser.

The Hippy poster is brighter, slicker, and more accessible than its
predecessor. Some of the methods used by poster designers in the
1890s have been revived – but they have been exaggerated and their
effect extended. In two posters from the 1960s, *Young Bloods* by
60 Victor Moscoso, a former student of Albers, and *Avalon Ballroom* by
64 Bob Schnepf, a dazzling effect is produced by juxtaposing comple-
mentary colours and confusing the spectator by allowing one pattern
to run into another. Two works by Will Bradley from the 1890s –
48 *The Chap Book* (1894–95) and *Victor Bicycles* – relied on a similar
element of confusion. In these designs the decoration of foliage and
the lettering are deliberately blended, so that it is quite difficult to
distinguish the message. One finds similar design ambiguities in the

60

work of Klimt. Neither in 1890 or 1960 is this confusion part of an attempt to make a private code for the initiated, but is in both cases an appeal to the senses rather than to reason. It is an attempt to defy interpretation. In presenting a confused pattern – which may seem a contradictory element when dealing with communications – the artist is saying, 'enjoy – let the effect ride over you – through you – use it – live it'. This attitude has even spread to criticism. Susan Sontag, in an essay written in 1964 and published in *Evergreen Review*, said:

> The aim of all commentary on art should now be to make works of art – and, by analogy, our own experience – more, rather than less real to us. The function of criticism should be to show 'how it is what it is,' even 'that it is what it is,' rather than to show 'what it means.'

54   VICTOR
MOSCOSO
*Hawaii Pop Rock
Festival* 1967

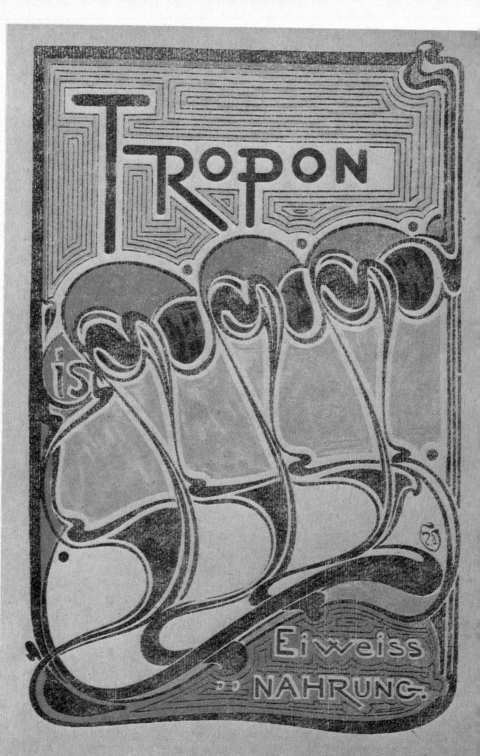

*56   PALLADINI *Medusa* 1968

◀ 55   HENRY VAN DE VELDE *Tropon* 1897

57 LOREN REHBOCK *Peace* 1967

58 PETER MAX *Love* 1967

This is the key to many poster designs of the 1960s – from the commercial posters advocating the 'consumer society' way of life at one end of the scale to the posters that suggest 'Love' or 'Peace' as a philosophy. Many of these designs rely on a sensuous appeal, and represent a break in the attitude that had been built up during the previous decades when the designer developed techniques of delivering clear, concise messages. In the 1960s the general public developed a technique of seeing without reading – even hearing without really listening. It is very much an attitude of mind: the messages come across through the senses generally.

In this way the Hippy poster is used to create an environment – in itself another manifestation of total art, as was Art Nouveau. The display of one Hippy poster is as ridiculous as placing one Art Nouveau article by itself as an object of taste. It can be done, but the true effect is achieved only if an entire environment is created:

57, 58

56

64

indeed, it is a way of life. Art Nouveau interiors reflected the architecture of the exterior and consisted of wallpaper, furniture, tableware, as well as all forms of decoration, including paintings and even clothing. Yet the Symbolist element in Art Nouveau reduced what might have been art as a total religion on a Wagnerian scale to the dimensions of a private cult. The Hippy poster has a more widespread effect because of the technical revolution in printing: the development of typesetting machines and the use of offset lithography. This has made possible the mass-production of colour work and low-key black and white photographic posters on a large scale. Legitimate publishing firms have been able to take advantage of this situation, but so also have the private presses.

It is now possible to collect rather crude reproductions of posters and poster-size photographs which seem to have an almost universal uniformity in Europe and the United States. Heroes such as Che 59 Guevara share the privacy of the domestic wall with W. C. Fields, designs by Beardsley and the posters of Toulouse-Lautrec. Mucha and Steinlen have reappeared alongside images of Marlene Dietrich, Brigitte Bardot and Karl Marx, together with many anonymous girls posing in the manner already established by Felicien Rops and

59   BOB SEIDEMANN
*Pig Pen, Organist of
the Grateful Dead
Band* 1966

PHOTO: PAUL KAGAN

TICKET OUTLETS

SAN FRANCISCO: PSYCEDELIC SHOP (HAIGHT-ASHBURY), CITY LIGHTS BOOKS (NORTH BEACH), THE TOWN SQUIRE (1318 POLK). BERKELEY: DISCOUNT RECORDS. SAUSALITO: TIDE'S BOOKSTORE. REDWOOD CITY: REDWOOD HOUSE OF MUSIC (700 WINSLOW). SAN MATEO: TOWN & COUNTRY MUSIC CENTER (25TH & EL CAMINO), LA MEL CAMERA & MUSIC (HILLSDALE AT 15TH). MENLO PARK: KEPLER'S BOOKS & MAGAZINES (825 EL CAMINO), SAN JOSE: DISCORAMA (435 NO. FIRST ST).

1967 FAMILY DOG PRODUCTIONS 837 GOUGH ST., San Francisco, Calif. 94102

60 VICTOR MOSCOSO
Young Bloods 1967

61 T. PRIVAT-LIVEMONT *Cercle Artistique de Schaerbeek* 1897

others. This constant bombardment of the senses has had the effect of producing a conditioned public whose tastes in visual experience are sophisticated. The effect of this poster craze on poster advertising generally has been to turn the commercial advertisement, and even the political poster, into a decorative mural and to link posters of the 1970s with the designs of the 1880s and 1890s almost a hundred years ago. An example of direct quotation appeared in Paul Christodoulou's poster (1967) for the Elliott Shoe Company in London. The sources, taken from the works of Beardsley, have been catalogued by the Print Room of the Victoria and Albert Museum, London, in a comprehensive list that shows how popular this sort of material had become in the 1960s:

62

The design contains elements from Beardsley's illustrations to The Wonderful History of Vergilius the Sorcerer, Salome – including

the Stomach Dance, The Woman in the Moon, Enter Herodias, the Eyes of Herod, The Toilette and the title page; Lysistrata haranguing the Athenian Women, Massalina returning from the bath, Neophyte and . . . the Black Art, the kiss of Judas, Sganarelle and the Beggar; the Pall Mall Magazine, cover design for the Yellow Book, Vols I and IV and a self portrait.

There are also sources of contemporary imagery in the posters of the 1960s, although this may be mixed with a style from the past. Science fiction, comics and mass-media references appear in many of the posters of the various Underground movements. In England, Mal Dean, John Hurford and Mike English have used mass-media references and Martin Sharp a series of phallic designs based on

comic-strip techniques. The American designer Peter Max, who 58
claimed that he wanted to redecorate the world, expresses the spirit
of many poster designers. A series of established billboard sites in the
United States, however, were suddenly covered in 1968 with a set
of mysterious designs that showed the head of a young man with a
great deal of hair – the caption merely read 'Get a haircut – Beautify
America'. Established advertising has not been slow to make use of
new methods. The most striking studio of art associates to appear in
the West is probably the American firm Push Pin whose *Almanack*
was first issued in 1954. Two of the founder members, Milton 63
Glaser and Seymour Chwast, showed their work together with their
associates in the Pavillon de Marsan in Paris in 1970, making yet
another link between the decorative advertisements of Europe in the
1880s and California in the 1960s.

However, the recent proliferation of posters and pseudo-posters,
in what has been described as a poster-mania, produces a mass of
material in which the vitality of the medium is weakened. At the
start of their book, *Après le Cubisme*, published in 1918, Amédée
Ozenfant and Le Corbusier quoted a statement by Voltaire that is as
significant in the 1970s as it was at the end of the First World War:
'The causes of decadence are facility in working well, weariness with
what is good and a taste for the bizarre.'

63   MILTON GLASER (Push Pin
     Studios) *Dylan* 1967

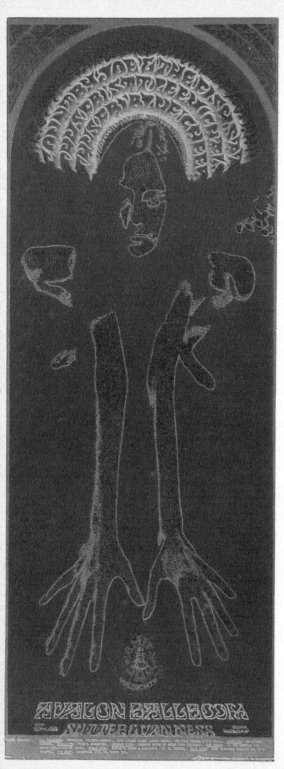

64 BOB SCHNEPF *Avalon Ballroom*
1967

BRADBURY THOMPSON *Flower Child* 1967

CHAPTER TWO

Modern and Professional

FORMAL ART MOVEMENTS

The term 'modern' has come to suggest a certain hollowness when applied to the arts – as though it represented a solution in design that time has quietly filed away with all the other styles. The twenties had an air of stylish optimism summed up in the title of Aldous Huxley's book *Brave New World*, and yet so much of its faded elegance has an element of what we now call 'camp'.

Two elements seem to have been at work: formal modern design   *68, 69*
and decorative modern. The first springs from the idea of function, which replaced the single word 'ornament' that had described the design of the nineteenth century. It represents that forward-looking design that links art with industry and the age of technology. The second element, decorative modern – regarded as a backward-looking style by Le Corbusier and his supporters – thrived in times of affluence, it represented the work of the individual and, as far as posters are concerned, was usually connected with painting.

Formal modern was to find a synthesis in the work of the Bauhaus, decorative modern in two periods – the first between the end of Art Nouveau in about 1900 and the rise of Bauhaus influence in   *267*
the early thirties, the second after the Second World War in the first decorative era of the consumer society. Inevitably some elements of formal design appear as decoration and this, as we shall see, was usually regarded as a compromise between the more rigid principles of design and the decorative manner that developed as a result of the emergence of new forms, The obvious example is the way in which the formal possibilities of Cubist design were turned into almost neo-classical decoration, not only by designers of posters but even by Picasso. The character of both those design elements that went to make up the new form of posters, as well as that of painting, appeared within a few years after 1900, although the dividing

73

◀ 66 JOOST SCHMIDT Poster for Bauhaus exhibition 1923

67 GISPEN *Rotterdam–South American Line* 1927

*68 NÖCKUR *Pressa* 1928. Compare th formal treatment with the more tradition approach of Ill. 69 (opposite)

line between the world of the nineteenth century and the new, mechanized world of the twentieth is often ascribed for convenience to the effect of the First World War. As far as design is concerned, or as far as art movements were affected by that catastrophic event, one can find only two major connections between the war and art. The Futurist movement seemed to anticipate the nature of mechanized warfare; and the Dadaists were born as a result of the despair produced by the hopelessness of it all. Otherwise, the many changes of style of the various art movements of the twentieth century have their foundations in the years between 1900 and 1917. The most important element in early twentieth-century design was the search for a new structural order, which was most apparent in what we call here 'formal art movements', such as Cubism, De Stijl and Constructivism.

As far as the public was concerned, the dates when these different art movements were made known occur between 1908 and 1917.

74

69   EHMCKE *Pressa* 1928

70   WLADIMIR LEBEDEW *Red Army and Navy* 1919

The first Cubist works of Picasso and Braque appeared in 1908.
In 1913 Malevich exhibited his first Suprematist work, *Quadrat*, a
black square on a white ground. In 1917 De Stijl, the Dutch progressive movement, was founded by Van Doesburg.

    Cubist paintings presented a new language of pictorial art which
tended towards abstraction. But however far the Cubists travelled
away from reality, they always returned to it, for Cubism was
basically an art concerned with the real. The Cubists, in fact, had
more to say about art and reality than many other painters who had
worked in the tradition of illusionistic representation since the
Renaissance. The Cubists made the artist's approach to reality both
intellectual and sensual. An artist did not necessarily record what he
could see of an object from one particular viewpoint – a convention
established by centuries of tradition in painting. Instead the Cubist
made an analysis of what he knew to be in front of him. Therefore,
an object was represented from all viewpoints simultaneously, and

in order to make this feat a possibility it became necessary to take reality to pieces and to re-assemble its fragments in a new structural form.

In this way, painting becomes more obviously a concept of the artist's intellect, and in the work of art a new language of form was developed to describe space. A painting produced in these terms has a life of its own. It has its own reality, which one is invited to explore mentally. In the past, one had been invited to 'take a walk' in a landscape with the help of various pictorial devices, like the road leading into the middle distance with subtle twists and turns. The Cubists rejected these methods of association, which were after all often merely sentimental responses to the illustration of a view. Instead, they substituted an artificial structure which was to be grasped with the mind and the senses as a fresh experience. In order to give the feel of a new reality, a great emphasis was laid on the tactile elements of the objects of the painting, either by implied surfaces of wood graining or marbling, or by literally incorporating pieces of material into the work. Collage, sand, parts of posters, lettering were pasted onto the work.

71 ROBERT BÉRENY Poster for Modiano cigarettes

72 WALTER KAMPMANN *Der Spiritismus* 1921

The work of art is therefore an independent entity that is itself a new reality. It is interesting that this movement in twentieth-century art was the direct result of a collaboration of personalities – Braque and Picasso. It is important to see that Cubism was both an intellectual and a sensory revolution: most writers on art underline the former, but painters have shown that the appeal to the senses and to the technical language of painting itself has been just as significant. To this double revolution one must therefore add a third element – the invention of the technical device of collage. Together, these developments were to be responsible for changes in the style of posters during the twentieth century.

In addition to the discoveries of Braque and Picasso, the effect of the work of Fernand Léger was to be reflected in posters. Léger's interest in the technical elements of modern civilization linked Cubist discoveries with the spirit of the new era. 'L'Esprit Nouveau' found expression in the writings and work of Amédée Ozenfant and Le Corbusier. Their precise treatment of objects and materials became known as the Purist Movement. This formal presentation of reality had clarity and directness – it was to be the principal influence on the applied arts everywhere; that of Léger was confined to France.

In *Après le Cubisme* (1918), Ozenfant and Le Corbusier stated: 'What we demand in art is precision. The necessity for order which alone can be effective has brought about a daring geometricization of the spirit which is entering more into all our activities. . . . Contemporary architecture exemplifies this process. Trams, railways, motor-cars, implements are all reduced to a rigorous form.' The authors felt that Cubism had, for example, in the neo-naturalism of Picasso's works of 1915–16, reverted to the old pictorial concepts of the past; certainly Picasso's later neo-classical work justifies this fear. The revolution of Cubism and the new technology of the age prompted Ozenfant to write later, in *Journey through Life* (1932), of '. . . the first Purist School 1918–26 which, dissenting from Cubism, was both a seeking after the principles of form and a protest against the arts of the drawing room.' In the same work, he also said that he wanted to find some means of making mass-produced paintings: he felt that genius lay in the all-important quality of invention. Problems of the

★73 CASSANDRE *Nicolas* 1935

★74 DRANSY *Dépôt Nicolas* 1922

loss of the personal touch in the execution of such works were of secondary importance. ' . . . if we really set out to look for mechanical or semi-automatic processes, some modern Gutenberg would very soon find them. Processes of this kind would do about eighty per cent of the work, and the master would do the rest by hand.'

73   At this point, designers in Paris such as Cassandre (1901–68) took up the language of the formal art movements and applied them to the advertising poster. The name 'Cassandre' was the pseudonym of Jean-Marie Moreau, who had been born in the Ukraine. By 1921 he was able to show that the mechanization of design – loved by the Futurists and by Moholy-Nagy – had in fact become a social reality, although he presented his mechanized compositions within the terms of Paris painting. In a colourful descriptive passage, he wrote that the poster had ceased to be a display but had become instead 'an announcing-machine' – a part of the repetitive process of mass-communication. In an introduction to a publication called *Publicité* (1928–29) he gives a poetic account of Paris, alive with the sights and sounds of modern advertising media and presided over by the illuminated Eiffel Tower.

99   Cassandre rarely used montage – *Wagon-bar* (1932) is a brilliant exception – but he simulated the effect of montage photographs in

78

carefully worked-out designs. At the age of twenty-four he produced his design for *L'Intransigeant* (1925), a work of almost classical purity, rigidly laid out on the Golden Section. A few years earlier, Ozenfant had written, 'Nous aurons aussi notre Parthénon, et notre époque est plus outillée que celle de Périclès pour réaliser l'idéal du perfection.' Cassandre's most acclaimed work has been his design *Étoile du Nord* **75** (1927), which combines a feeling for the new technology and a comlete faith in its function. One senses the inevitable reliability of the railway system and the vast spaces that the track covers so directly.

*75 CASSANDRE
Étoile du Nord 1927

The set of three posters that Cassandre designed for Dubonnet (1934) are good examples of the use of precise arrangement in the popular idiom. Cassandre expresses movement here in the way a film sequence develops a series of events: the three panels of the poster show three stages through which a man is seen to anticipate, savour and finally become attracted to the apéritif. The automaton-like figure becomes suffused by the drink, which also causes his eye to roll around, in the accepted reaction to this condition. The letters that spell out 'Dubonnet' are also gradually suffused in the same way, implying, in French, a gradual acceptance of something, something that is good, something that is also the name of the product. Such a decorative and humorous use of the clean lines of Purism shows how the formal possibilities of the new design could lead on into decorative treatment. In *Dubonnet* Cassandre joined other designers in Paris in the thirties whose work contributed to the decorative style of that era, and to which we must return later. At the moment we are concerned with that formalized approach to design which Cassandre derived from the abstract movements in the arts and which led to posters like his *L'Intransigeant*.

In 1933 he summed up his attitude towards the role of the poster designer in this way:

> It is difficult to determine the status of the poster among the pictorial arts. Some reckon it as a department of painting, which is mistaken, others place it among the decorative arts and I believe

76 CASSANDRE *Dubo–Dubon–Dubonnet* 1934

they are no less mistaken. The poster is neither a painting nor a theatrical backdrop but something different, although it often makes use of the means offered by the one or the other. The poster demands utter resignation on the part of the artist. He must not assert his personality. If he does so it would be contrary to his rights.

Painting is an end in itself. The poster is only a means to an end, a means of communication between the dealer and the public, something like a telegraph. The poster designer plays the part of a telegraph official: he does not initiate news: he merely dispenses it. No one asks him for his opinion, he is only required to bring about a clear, good and exact connection.

In making this statement, Cassandre is preparing the way for the emergence of the professional communications expert. In Paris, the national home of Cubism, it was natural that French designers would develop their ideas from that movement or from other local movements – such as Purism – that stemmed from it. In other countries, movements such as De Stijl and Constructivism, which in the early stages of their development had looked to Cubism for pictorial reference, later applied these discoveries in ways that were to have a more direct influence on poster design than Cubism itself.

In 1915 Mondrian returned to Holland from Paris, where he had been associated with Cubism. He developed the new formulae to a more disciplined conclusion than that reached by Cubist work, which later became decorative. As a result his influence, and that of Van Doesburg, who founded De Stijl in 1917, extended the initial, 265 breakthrough of the Cubists to influence and transform the way we now live. Mondrian wrote in 1942:

While Neo-Plasticism now has its own intrinsic value, as painting and sculpture, it may be considered as a preparation for a future architecture. It can complete existing new architecture in the way of establishment of pure relationships and pure colour. Actually it is an expression of our modern age. Modern industry and progressive technics show parallel if not equal developments. Neo-Plasticism should not be considered a personal conception. It is the

77 PIET ZWART *Either* 1930

78 OTTO BAUMBERGER *Forster* 1930

logical development of all art, ancient and modern; its way lies
open to everyone as a principle to be applied.

The effect of the formal art movements on our environment is clearly
stated by Mondrian in this quotation, and future work at the
Bauhaus, and in the 1950s in the movement known as *Die neue
Sachlichkeit* (New Objectivity) in Switzerland, shows how the early
achievements of De Stijl were expanded and applied. But before we
examine these two areas of design, there are further developments in
connection with the formal arts that spring more closely from the
Dutch movement. De Stijl design was restricted, in its orthodox
form, to the use of primary colours and simple square or rectangular
shapes. The Dutch designer, Piet Zwart, born in 1885, has been responsible for some of the most adventurous typographical work
based freely on this formal discipline.

Hendrik Werkman (1882–1945) developed the use of printers'
materials – inks, rollers and assorted type – to create compositions

which he called *druksels* – from the Dutch word 'to print'. Word pictures had been used by Marinetti and Apollinaire, and one can quote a precedent such as 'The Mouse's Tale' in Lewis Carroll's *Alice in Wonderland*. In Werkman's designs, the arrangement of different typefaces conveyed the effects of collage and montage that other contemporary art movements had achieved. The letters themselves 100 formed the image – an idea that the Cubists and Dadaists had been quick to understand – except that in Werkman's designs the process of using type in painting had been reversed. Braque and Boccioni had used lettering in their easel paintings as a means of introducing an element of reality. Werkman, on the other hand, 'painted' with type. Posters using type in this way expressed pictorial patterns instead of decorative but straightforward arrangements. An interesting development of Werkman's experiments is seen in Robert Indiana's poster *Noel* (1969) – one of a series of variations dealing with the 103 relationship of large single letters. The unusual achievement of Werkman was cut short when he was killed during the occupation of the Netherlands during the Second World War, and much of his

JAN TSCHICHOLD *Graphic Design* 1927

80 OSKAR SCHLEMMER *Grosse Brücken Revue* 1926

original work was destroyed during the Liberation. In the Netherlands an imaginative use of formal design in poster layout has been continued in the work of Willem Sandberg and Wim Crouwel.

One of the most significant single influences on 'formal' design has been that of Jan Tschichold, who was born in 1902 and who graduated from the Leipzig Academy of Book Design. In *Asymmetric Typography*, published in 1935, he writes (trans. Ruari Maclean):

> The connection between 'abstract' painting and the new typography does not lie in the use of 'abstract' forms but in similarity of working methods. In both, the artist must first make a scientific study of his available materials and then, using contrast, forge them into an entity. . . . The works of 'abstract' art are subtle creations of order out of simple, contrasting elements. Because this is exactly what typography is trying to do, it can derive stimulus and instruction from a study of such paintings, which communicate the visual forms of the modern word and are the best teachers of visual order.

81   BORIS PRUSAKOV *I Hurry to See Khaz Push* 1927

82　EL LISSITZKY Poster for Russian
Exhibition, Zürich 1929

83　G. KLUTSIS *Transport Achievement
of the First Five-Year Plan* 1929

In his poster for *Phoebus Palast* (1927), Tschichold uses photography
as an 'abstract' element. A shot from the film is cut into a circle which
is balanced with an oblique line. This, in turn, is set at right angles to
lines of sans serif type. The shot, incidentally, is of Buster Keaton,
whose props in this instance consist of cannon balls and railway track
so that the shapes in the still are repeated in the total design of the
poster.

Keaton appears again, with his stony expression staring from the
elements of formal design – this time in a poster by the Stenberg
brothers in Russia. Formal elements are used decoratively in this film
poster, but the contribution from the Constructivist movement towards precise 'abstract' poster design was considerable. In her book,
The Great Experiment: Russian Art 1863–1922, Camilla Gray-
Prokofieva notes the connection between the work of Alexander
Rodchenko (1891–1956) and that of Dziga Vertov of *The Man with* 85
the Ciné Camera and *Kino-Pravda*, and also the effect of the early films
of Eisenstein. His use of camera angles is apparent in the posters for
Battleship Potemkin. Eisenstein's sophisticated use of montage is also
reflected in a poster such as *Russische Ausstellung* (1929) by Eleazar 82

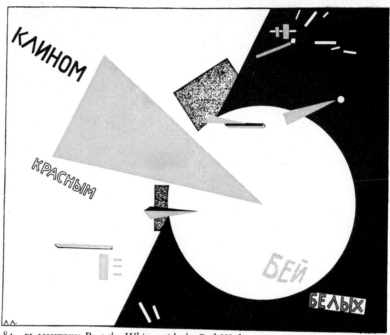

84 EL LISSITZKY *Beat the Whites with the Red Wedge* 1919

Markovich – known as El Lissitzky (1890–1941). In this poster
Lissitzky does not make use of a photograph as Tschichold had done
in *Phoebus Palast*, but instead creates a new reality through montage.
Lissitzky was also the first to use the device of the 'photogram' as a
poster – for *Pelikan Ink* (1924) – but his most direct use of formal design in a poster can be seen in the work, *Beat the Whites with the Red
Wedge* (1919–20). In this poster he uses simple elements – sharp, aggressive shapes, circles, and the direct impact of black, red and white.
He later made an illustrated accompaniment to Mayakovsky's poem,
For Reading Out Loud (1923), and in *The Story of Two Squares* produced a work that is pure visual communication in abstract terms.

Malevich described the nature of this new language when he
wrote of another movement – Suprematism:

> The forms of Suprematism are imbued with the same forces as the
> living forms of nature. Suprematism is a new form of pictorial

86
84

86

realism, a realism which is purely formal because there are no mountains, no sky and no water. Each true form is a world in itself. And each pure unmarked surface has more life than a drawn or painted face with a pair of eyes and a smile.

The styles produced by the various art movements during the early years of the twentieth century left their mark on poster design at the time, but the general effect of the new formalism was consolidated and directed in Germany. In 1922 Van Doesburg invited Moholy-Nagy, Richter, Lissitzky, Arp, Tzara and Schwitters to a conference at Weimar, the original home of the Bauhaus, which was then in its fourth year. The confrontation of personalities was perhaps less fruitful than the idea that such connections were possible. Much more significant was the proximity of the Bauhaus itself, which rapidly came to represent the centre for the new spirit. This is not to say that there was ever a 'Bauhaus Style', but rather that the elements brought together by that school represented a body of alternative work to the universally admired School of Paris. In Weimar a group of brilliant European artists, including Feininger, Itten, Klee, Kandinsky, Schlemmer, Moholy-Nagy, Albers and others, under *80*

*85 DZIGA VERTOV *The Man with the Ciné Camera* 1928

86 EL LISSITZKY *Pelikan Ink* (photogram) 1924

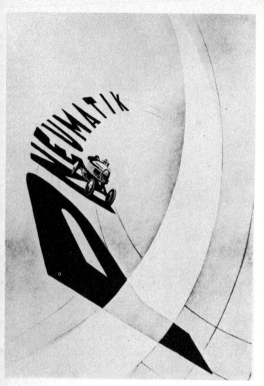

87 LASZLO MOHOLY-NAGY *Pneumatik* 1926

88 LASZLO MOHOLY-NAGY *Militarismus* (photomontage) 1924

the direction of Walter Gropius, brought their intelligence to bear on the new discoveries. Equally important, they aimed at a universal participation in artistic experience based on the old formula of the medieval guild relationship of master and apprentice – but in terms of the twentieth century and mass-production.

Within the staff of the Bauhaus itself, it is necessary to distinguish between those, such as Klee, Feininger, Itten and Kandinsky, whose work one might say belonged to a spiritual area of expression, and Moholy-Nagy, whose work places him alongside Lissitzky, Malevich and members of De Stijl. It is with these latter names, linked with the new elements of the age – one in spirit with society, social system and architecture – that the most significant influence of the Bauhaus on poster design is to be found. Moholy-Nagy understood that the new techniques of the cinema – montage, trick

87

88

88

photography, camera angle – could all be used as creative elements in posters. If one compares the effective though 'dead' montage of a work by, say, Hannah Hoch with the related elements of Moholy-Nagy's *Circus and Variety* poster, one can see that a new 'living' reality could be created out of the images of still photography.

Various art movements, then, converged in Germany in the early twenties and it is in this area and during this crucial period of reconstruction after the First World War that the foundations for an

integration of design and painting were laid. In 1924 Moholy-Nagy wrote:

> Whereas typography, from Gutenberg up to the first posters, was merely a (necessary) intermediary link between the content of a message and the recipient, a new stage of development began with the first posters . . . one began to count on the fact that form, size, colour and arrangement of the typographical material (letters and signs) contain a strong visual impact. The organization of these possible visual effects gives a visual validity to the content of the message as well; this means that by means of printing the content is also defined pictorially. . . . This is the essential task of visual-typographical design.

Moholy-Nagy was mainly responsible for the new elements in Bauhaus typography and advertising techniques from 1923 until the beginning of the Dessau period (1925), when the Bauhaus had to move from its original home in Weimar. Development of a specific Bauhaus type began in about 1923. It was derived in part from the work of Schwitters and also of Van Doesburg – thus bringing together ideas from Dada and De Stijl. Moholy-Nagy initiated the idea of type without capitals, which was implemented by Herbert Bayer (1924).

66   In 1929 and 1930 the influence of Joost Schmidt on Bauhaus poster design led to a development of posters into three dimensions as exhibition structures. The development of a combined commercial art and photographic department in Berlin under Peterhans stressed the exhibition-stand photographic poster in Bauhaus design (1932). The Bauhaus existed at Weimar from 1919 until 1925, at Dessau from 1925 to 1932 and in Berlin during 1933, when the Nazis insisted that changes should be made in the staff and programme so that it would conform to the ideals of National Socialism. The Bauhaus was then re-established in the United States. The formal art movements which had started in Europe had a direct influence, through the teaching of the Bauhaus, throughout the world. Walter
267   Allner and Herbert Bayer, among others, continued the work of the Bauhaus in America after its 'expulsion' from Europe. The Bauhaus

signalled not only a change in design, but of the place of design within society and so ultimately of society itself.

The country that followed the developments of the Bauhaus most closely was Switzerland. Switzerland was removed from the economic depression, which had begun in the United States, and later became encircled by the Second World War. The disastrous six years of war did affect Switzerland, but not in the way that other countries were affected. There was no real outlet in Switzerland for advertising, and it became necessary to cultivate an artistic organization in order to continue graphic work. This was achieved on a national scale by the Ministry of the Interior. Switzerland, well known for its precise craftsmanship, also has a distinguished history of design. Among Swiss poster artists of international rank one can number Grasset, Steinlen and Amiet – and, more recently, Matter, *178* Max Bill and Leupin.

Two elements in Swiss poster design which originate from the 1920s became known as 'New Objectivity'. They consisted, on the one hand, of a realistic image – usually very precise – of the object together with simple, formal lettering, and on the other, a two-dimensional simplification of the object reduced to a symbol. This led to the abstract poster, which, as it became accepted, was a step forward in the development of an international language of communication symbols – a necessary step among nations that have become increasingly interdependent through technology.

An example of abstract poster design that stems from these developments is the series of works designed by Müller-Brockmann for concert performances in the Zürich Tonhalle (*c.* 1960). Writing of these posters, the artist said:

The concert posters done before 1960 were designed with strict formal elements and simple design media. They were intended as the symbolic expression of the innate laws of music. The thematic, dynamic, rhythmic and metrical factors in music were illustrated by corresponding optical forms and form sequences, and the tone colours by the selection of visual colours interpreting the emotional content of the composition concerned in each case.

91

The designs and colours of these posters were largely selected on emotional, subjective grounds and considerations. However, it was then felt desirable to restore to the posters the greatest possible power of imparting information, without secondary objectives or decoration. This entailed dropping colour and working purely by typographical methods.

The concert posters from the period subsequent to 1960 represent a conscious departure from formally symbolic shapes and a return to poster advertising based on pure typography. These tasks previously assigned to design forms – the illustration of dynamic rhythm, tone colour and so on – have now been taken over by typography. This enables the available space to be integrated and brought into rhythm. Lettering applied in various colours and integrated logically can produce a poster laden with musical atmosphere and tension.

The example of Switzerland has been underlined because of the substantial contribution from its artists to formal design; but by the 1960s there were also important examples in other countries – Italy, for example. But it is necessary first to retrace our steps to the Decorative arts of 1910.

90 JOSEF MÜLLER-BROCKMANN Concert poster for Zürich Townhall 1960

91 THORN PRIKKER *Dutch Exhibition in Krefeld* 1903

DECORATIVE ART MOVEMENTS

It is by now a commonplace observation that great exhibitions commemorating art movements usually announce that the style is dead and that by the time the official organizations have managed to accumulate enough examples and funds to mount the display, creative talent is busy elsewhere. In 1900, an Exposition in Paris proclaimed the beginning of the end of Art Nouveau. In 1925 the Exposition of Decorative Arts in Paris revealed the climax of another chapter in the history of design, although the effects of twentieth-century decorative design were to continue down the scale through successive waves of imitation until the advancing tide of new decoration from the United States introduced fresh elements of style in the 1940s.

93

92   An example of posters on display in Germany 1917

Decorative poster design in Europe from 1910 until 1939 seems to have proceeded in different countries according to the local elements of decorative design. For example, in Germany the delicate pattern of Secessionist design produced one element, the heavy shapes of Munich Jugendstil another – and both of these appear constantly in German posters. In England, the most significant posters derived from the simple, flat patterns of the posters of the Beggarstaff Brothers. In France, the colour of Les Fauves, the fashion designs of couturiers such as Paul Poiret, and the work of Jean Cocteau prepared the way for a decorative style that was further enlivened by the many influences that gravitated to Paris, which remained, during this period, the principal art centre of the world. The visit of the Ballets Russes to Paris is just one example. Picasso designed 'Cubist' decorations for Diaghilev's *Parade*: particularly significant are the set of drawings showing the metamorphosis of a sandwich-board man wearing his posters into a Cubist pattern of still-life and portrait, together with the lettering and picture-plane of

94

the poster. That one of the founders of Cubism could make use of his discoveries in this decorative way shows that the lament on the part of the Purists – that the work of the Cubists lacked 'precision' – was justified. The decorative possibilities of Cubist discoveries also contributed to poster design, although in a way that was quite different from the austere influence of the formal art movements.

The 'angularity' that one associates with so much 'Art Déco' is found in the fashion designs of artists such as Boussingault in his drawings for the fashion designer Paul Poiret (an example can be found in *La Gazette du Bon Ton* in 1914). Poiret himself detested Cubism and its austerity, and we must therefore accept that we have two distinct lines of development in poster designs between 1910 and 1939, one stemming from Cubist abstraction (but even more precise), and the other, based on decorative angular patterns that also take in Cubist developments. Our division of the 'modern' into

93 LUPUS *Rikola Bücher* 1924

formal and decorative therefore seems justified by the very real antipathy that existed between artists at the time. Le Corbusier despised the so-called decorative arts – an article in his *L'Esprit Nouveau* (1924) by Paul Boulard condemned 'phoney-cubism', laid out by the kilometre. (He attacked Cassandre's first widely dis-

95 tributed poster, *Au Bucheron*, as a 'gros messieur' in the tradition of Meissonier.) Corbusier in his turn seems to have been persecuted at the Decorative Arts Exhibition of 1925 when his pavilion, already confined to a poor site, was surrounded by an 18-foot-high wall. The first prize that an international jury had awarded him was vetoed by the French member of the jury.

The posters of Cassandre were derived partly from the work of
75 Purist designs – as we have seen already in his *Etoile du Nord* and
99 *Wagon-bar* – and partly from neo-classical decoration, as is evident in his posters *Grèce* (1933) and *Angleterre* (1934) – a more decorative development than Cubism, which appeared also in the work of Braque as well as that of Picasso. Cassandre later made designs in the United States for *Harper's Bazaar* and also turned his attention to theatre décor. His style also relates to that of other poster designers in Paris at that time, notably Jean Carlu (born 1900), who, in turn, also helped to spread the Paris style in the United States, where posters and billboards tended to be realistic photographs, paintings from these or cartoon gags enlarged to poster size. In his poster, *America's Answer – Production* (1945), Carlu displayed some of the devices of the Decorative Arts in Paris. The title lettering of the poster is displayed across the work. Beyond this, a large gloved hand in the form of a symbol grasps a wrench which is fastened around the first 'o' of the word 'production' as though it were a nut. In this way the typography is made part of an implied picture from reality. This device is typical of Carlu's earlier work, which always has strength and simplicity: the neon version (1935) of his poster *Cuisine Élec-*
96 *trique* shows these characteristics. He made other excursions into mixed media poster form, including work for Osram, Martel and, with Claude Lemeunier, *Cordon Bleu*.

Paul Colin, who exerted a great influence both through his work and through his design school, is represented here by a study

94 FRANK NEWBOULD *Ventnor* 1922

for the poster *Bal Nègre*. This brilliant design clearly relates the 104
poster to decorative painting of the time. It also presents the new
entertainment world of Paris that had succeeded the *café chantant*
as the subject of the music and variety poster. The work of musicians
and singers such as Josephine Baker represented a continuation of
the cosmopolitan life of Paris as reflected in the posters of the
1890s. There is, however, the important change technically in the
transference of ideas from canvas to print. In the work of Cassandre,
Carlu and Colin, surface marks, whether of brush or of collage, are
usually invisible in the immaculate poster-prints. Even hand-
lettering is indistinguishable from type. The effect of photo-montage
is simulated: there is none of the 'artist's handwriting' that one finds,

97

95 CASSANDRE *Au Bucheron* 1923

96 JEAN CARLU *Cuisine Électrique* 1935

97 JEAN DUPAS *London Passenger Transport Board* 1933

*98   PAULET THEVENEZ Poster for Jacques Dalcroze's system of eurhythmics 1924

for example, in an Expressionist poster. This seems to be a concession towards the mass-production precision of the time, implying that decoration itself was leaning towards formalism. The appearance of the actual painting surfaces of the works of Constructivists and De Stijl artists may have been the obvious source – as they were to be for the painters of hard-edge compositions in the 1960s. Another, less obvious, source for an 'impersonal' technique of execution was the work of Dali and Tanguy.

Posters such as *Cointreau* (1926) by A. Mercier; *Mlle Rahra* (*c.* 1927) by Bernard Becan; Pierre Fix-Masseau's *Le Transport Gratuit* and Paulet Thevenez's poster of 1924 are all typical works that relate to the 'Art Déco' style. Jean Dupas's *London Passenger Transport Board*, from the thirties, is characteristic of his paintings, which are so much a part of the period. The fashion designs of Georges Lepape that appear in the *Gazette du Bon Ton* and *Les Choses de Poiret* (1911) – two sources that are indispensable for those interested in the design of this era – are also reflected in his poster, *Soirée de Gala pour L'Enfance*. The influence of Paris design on

109

98

97

99

99   CASSANDRE *Wagon-bar* 1932 ▶

100   HENDRIK WERKMAN *Composition with Letter O* 1927 ▶

Cⁱᵉ INTᵉ ᴬᴸᵉ DES WAGONS LITS

A.M. CASSANDRE

GRANDS RÉSEAUX DE CHEMINS DE FER FRANÇAIS

RESTAUREZ-VOUS
AU
WAGON-BAR
consommations ~ petits repas
A PEU DE FRAIS

decorative posters lasted from before the First World War until well after the Second, as in the sensitive work of Picart-Le-Doux and Nathan-Garamond. In France the Union de l'Affiche Française furnished printers, designers and agents with a form of organization which other countries lacked. Posters in France, however, did not have so wide a dissemination in the community as they did, for example, in England.

Many French designers were commissioned by British organizations, such as London Transport, Shell Oil and Imperial Airways, to make posters. However, many English designs still related the poster to its smaller ancestor – the printed page. Painters made designs which were well reproduced and frequently accompanied by captions, as if they were intended for a book. The idea that the poster should be the 'art gallery of the street' suggested that artwork should come from eminent painters as well as 'commercial' artists. Unfortunately this resulted all too often in a respectable, tasteful series of harmless views or jolly travel posters that may be characteristic of the period but which hardly added to the power of poster design. The most interesting posters came from designers such as Tom Purvis, *London and North Eastern Railway*, or Frank
94 Newbould, *Ventnor* (1922), whose simple, flat pattern-making recalls the work of Pryde and Nicholson.

In spite of the 'good taste' that this patronage brought to the form of the English poster (in much the same way as radio developed under the British Broadcasting Corporation), one has to realize that monopoly brought certain benefits. The work of Frank Pick for London Transport and Jack Beddington for Shell are important contributions to the spread of poster display and general design co-ordination. The outstanding work in England by the American designer McKnight Kauffer was recognized by Frank Pick, to whom Kauffer dedicated his book, *The Art of the Poster*, in 1924. Kauffer came to Europe after seeing the 1913 Armory Show in New York.
108 His design, *Flight of Birds* (1919), which was used for the *Daily Herald*, is typical of his grasp of geometrical decoration. This is also demonstrated in his poster, *London Museum* (1922), for Underground Railways. His designs represent a compromise between the formal

and decorative art movements. In his book he admitted that few of the posters of his time were ever 'designed either with "cubistic" or "futuristic" finality' – two adjectives which he complained were applied indiscriminately by the public of 1924 to anything unusually modern.

Another designer in England whose work showed similar stylistic connections was Frederick Charles Herrick, in his poster *Royal Mail* 101 (his was the only English poster in the Paris Decorative Arts Exhibition of 1925). The painter Edward Wadsworth, whose poster advertising *Englische Graphik* in 1923 showed an appreciation of the effects of a startling pattern, provides a link with the English avant-garde. Similarly Aubrey Hammond's *Evie de Ropp* (1923) and V.L. Danvers's *Bobby's* (1928) are characteristic period pieces. 102

No less significant in the history of posters were the designs from Austria and Germany. A study of the pages of the magazine *Das Plakat*, issued from 1910 until 1921, reveals a body of work just as remarkable as that produced in Paris, and representing a consistent

101 FREDERICK CHARLES HERRICK *Royal Mail c.* 1921   102 V. L. DANVERS *Bobby's* 1928

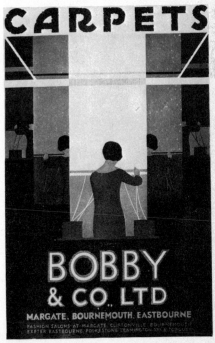

NO
ELL

NEIMAN
MARCUS

ROBERT INDIANA 1966

104 PAUL COLIN *Bal Nègre*

◀ ★103 ROBERT INDIANA *Noel* 1969

development from Secessionist and Jugendstil design. An additional stylistic element appeared with a return to the decorative interpretation of realism. The principal exponents of this new style, if one can group together individual artists, were Ludwig Hohlwein (1874–1949) and Lucian Bernhard (b. 1883). Both artists made use of the characteristic flat pattern and simplified design that had become the essence of powerful poster imagery from Toulouse-Lautrec to variations in other countries (such as the work of Pryde and Nicholson in England). In his poster *Hermann Scherrer* (1911), Hohlwein presents a realistic concept executed with an economy of means. The shadows, clearly marked, are in fact the ground of the poster. The shadow, itself an innovation in flat designs – one does not often find shadows used in Art Nouveau posters – here becomes a decorative element, although its actual shape is dictated by observation. By exaggerating the contrast of light and shade the artist implies relief in a two-dimensional work, which is, however, flattened by the patterns of the textiles illustrated in the poster. Hohlwein used flat areas of tweed or tartan which he frequently 'laid' across the design – not literally, although they very well could have been. It is interesting that Picasso was at the same time laying the piece of simulated cane on his *Still-life with Cane Seat* (1911–12).

105   LUCIAN BERNHARD *Prieste*

Hohlwein first used this method in 1908 in his posters *Confection Kahl* and *Kunstgewerbehaus Gebrueder Wollweber*. Another example of Hohlwein's technique can be seen in *Audi-Automobil* (1912).

It is interesting to see that the large revolutionary posters from Cuba in 1969 have revived his methods. The realistic image produced by this use of isolated patches of colour was given more conventional treatment by Hohlwein in posters of a straightforward manner such as *Norddeutscher Lloyd Bremen* (1912). In his later posters, Hohlwein moved away from the decorative quality in his work and made designs with loose brush-strokes that give them the feeling of being 'paintings'. His subject-matter (the middle class in evening dress or the colonial official) became very popular not only in Germany but also in the United States. Carl Moos shows a similar approach to Hohlwein's earlier style in *Lessing and Co. Cigarettenfabrik* (1910).

261

Lucian Bernhard, who was born in Vienna and studied at the Munich Academy, now lives in New York. His posters show a distinctive, decorative quality, rounded and luxuriant, based on reality – descriptive, yet each a complete work, as in *Berliner Sitzmöbil-Industrie* (1905?), *Mampes-Liköre* (1909), *Luce Borch* (1914),

105 *Manoli Gibson-Girl* (1913-14). *Priester* shows his use of the single object, presented, in this case, on a monumental scale. His poster for *Verkadee's Biskwie* (1919) illustrates the form of the 'Sach-Plakat' (fact-poster) formulated in 1905 – it is a still-life realized in meticulous detailed accuracy, clear, precise and unemotional. Throughout his career Bernhard has shown particular interest in the use of lettering: a number of typefaces have been named after him.

107 Other decorative posters from Germany are *Vogue Parfüm* by Jupp Wiertz, *Marouf* (*c.* 1935) by Marfurt, Fritz Bucholz's cigarette

110 poster design *Caba* (*c.* 1924) from the studio of Hans Neumann and

106 *Jacobinier* (*c.* 1927) by Julius Klinger. The anonymous design

108   E. MCKNIGHT KAUFFER *Flight of birds* (design for a poster) 1919

109   JEAN A. MERCIER *Cointreau* 1926

129   *Imperator* (*c.* 1914) also has a special quality that is not found in the designs from Paris. Posters by designers such as Gipkens, Gulbransson and Preetorius add to the remarkable German contribution, which also reflected Cubist ideas – for example, in the posters of
67, 133   Kampmann, Gispen and Dolliers (*c.* 1915).

THE PROFESSIONAL DESIGNER

While the modern art movements had contributed stylistic changes to the art of poster design, another factor had been developing which was to affect the place of posters in advertising generally and, ultimately, to affect their style as well. The importance of the professional graphic designer had emerged from the interchange between the fine and applied arts at the turn of the century, which, in turn, had derived from the original design movements of the nineteenth century.

112   SAUL BASS *Bunny Lake is Missing* 1965   113   KEIICHI TANAAMI *Men's Weekly*

The liaison between industry and the designer had an early precedent in the commission that the firm Tropon gave Van de Velde in the 1890s; this resulted in the famous poster of 1898, as well as Van de Velde's designs for packaging, and a prospectus. Similarly Peter Behrens was commissioned to design, for the Allgemeine Elektrizitätsgesellschaft, everything from the notepaper heading to the building itself – an early example of complete design co-ordination. In England, Frank Pick was responsible for developing a series of design elements for London Underground Railways that gave the amalgamated transport system of that metropolis a co-ordinated pattern. For the same organization Edward Johnston designed a typeface in 1916, which was the first sans serif type to be cut from new designs in the twentieth century. It is still in use and makes an interesting comparison with the same, although inde-pendently developed, use of sans serif at the Bauhaus.

111

EVÏE
de
ROPP

AUBREY HAMMOND. 1922.

ST MARY'S of the LAKE
by the
NORTH SHORE LINE

An inspired use of design, that extended throughout the advertising of a single product and introduced a number of outstanding visual innovations, was the series of decorative posters and murals made by Charles Loupot for the firm of St Raphael in France. Following the anonymous design, which appeared in 1928, showing two waiters bearing St Raphael Apéritif, Loupot produced a number of variations in 1938 which made a formal pattern out of the design. During the years that followed, until 1957, his work – later carried out from the Atelier Loupot – developed into designs for large painted wall-space, breaking up the formal patterns into fragments. These were distributed in any given locality, often appearing as giant abstract shapes with no acknowledgment to St Raphael; but the simple colour combination of red, white and black, and the sweeping triangular shapes, made their identity obvious. The most interesting part of this campaign was the establishment of design in an environment – free from the conventional hoarding or billboard if necessary, and relating one mural to another over a wide landscape. The same design was also used on cars, and buses: even to the extent of linking the movement of the bus to set the elements of the design in motion.

118–124

116   DONALD BRUN *Gauloises* 1965

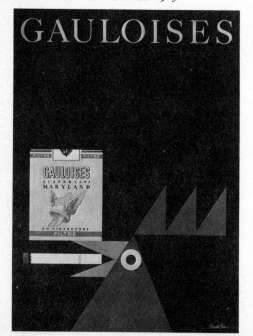

117   JACQUI MORGAN *Electric Circus* 1969

★118–24   CHARLES LOUPOT and ATELIER *St Raphael*
1938–57

115

126 LUCIAN BERNHARD *Stiller* 1907–08

◀ 125 LUDWIG HOHLWEIN *Hermann Scherrer* 1911

127 GIOVANNI PINTORI
Olivetti 82 Diaspron

In Italy, Adriano Olivetti, the first advertising manager of that company in 1928 (he later became president), was responsible for
138 design co-ordination. Marcello Nizzoli not only provided designs for posters but also for Olivetti typewriters. Among other designers employed by the company were distinguished artists such as Bruno
127 Munari and Giovanni Pintori. In a statement accompanying the Olivetti exhibition *Concept and Form*, shown during the Edinburgh Festival of 1970, there is this comment on the relation of the designer to industry:

> The artist who is merely consulted by industry remains himself, just as the industry remains unchanged. A transient relationship could not define the two parties except momentarily, even though the relationship does begin with mutual attraction and perhaps leaves some trace. The depth and dynamism of industrial form spring from an accumulation of such relationships – in other words a cultural policy.

Naturally the form of a poster, when it comes not only from an industrial designer but from one who is playing a part in the overall

118

128   M. DUDOVICH *Olivetti* ▸

129   ANONYMOUS *Imperator* (from *Das Plakat*) *c.* 1914

130   PAUL SCHEURICH *Dennerts Lexikon*

policy of design, is bound to be different from that of a poster designed by an independent artist. Posters reflecting the spirit of the
product became a part of advertising display in the 1950s.

Professional design consultants, agencies, groups of studios
and companies, and the establishment of graphic-design courses for
students suggest a degree of organization that might have stifled ex-
perimentation. From the mass of tasteful and sophisticated advertising material which at times seemed to have an international
uniformity, various names of special importance appeared during the
1960s: Push Pin, founded in California under the direction of Milton
Glaser and Seymour Chwast; the distinguished partnership in London of Theo Crosby, Alan Fletcher and Colin Forbes; and the work
of Albrecht Ade and the Department of Graphic Design at the

259
131

131 CROSBY/FLETCHER/FORBES *Pirelli* 1960s

Werkkunstschule, Wuppertal. The work of the professional artist-businessman is, of course, in the great tradition of artists who are also able to delegate their work, an image established long before 'the outcast artist' became the criterion of integrity.

The position of the professional designer was summed up in the introduction to *Neue Grafik*, a design magazine which, during its short life, represented the views of professional designers – with a particular emphasis on formal design work: 'The modern designer is no longer the servant of industry, no longer an advertising draftsman or an original poster artist; he acts independently, planning and creating the whole work, informing it with the full weight of his personality so that very often his design determines the actual form of the product with which he has been dealing.' These words anticipate the development of design co-ordination, a system of unified graphic design in any corporation, relating also to the shape of the product and including any poster advertising. This would seem to be the logical conclusion for the role of the professional designer. However, the body of professional designers were themselves largely responsible for the form that commercial advertising took in posters in the period of decorative design, the forties and fifties.

135

247

132   RUDOLPH ALTRICHTER *ATD . . . (A Small Nation also Wants to Live)* 1964

DIE GUTE BELOHNUNG

Pathécolor

Location et Vente de films et appareils Pathé frères. 104 rue de Paris. Vincennes

133 DOLLIERS *The Good Reward c.* 1916

134 EUGENE MAX CORDIER *German State
Railways* 1955

VISITEZ LA BAVIÈRE

CHEMIN DE FER
FÉDÉRAL
ALLEMAND

A change in style in the decorative arts appeared in the 1940s and 1950s. In Europe, an amalgamation of formal and decorative styles, developed in the Scandinavian countries, was imitated with less success in other areas. In the United States, a more flamboyant version of the same amalgamation appeared in the 'streamline' decoration of automobiles and in architecture. The significant distinction between the two areas lay in the way the new style was adapted by the imitators in each case. In Europe, the minimal elements of design used in work based on ideas from De Stijl or Constructivism too

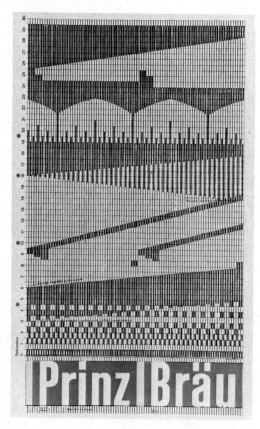

*135 KARL GERSTNER
Computer
programming sheet
for Prinzl Bräu c.
1968

136   F. H. K. HENRION *Go Super National Benzole* 1960

often degenerated into mere austerity in countries that had suffered economically as a result of the war. In the United States, industrial and technological expansion led to the development of popular design elements. The two broad areas of expression on each side of the Atlantic produced a new style, as diverse as Art Nouveau. In Britain this New World seemed less 'brave' than its predecessor in the twenties: the style was described, rather flatly, as 'contemporary'.

The desperate attempt to stay modern yet be acceptable to a new consumer society – in some cases re-building its shattered towns – led to a form of mannerism. That term, as applied to sixteenth-century art, suggested elements of paradox and contradiction that were the product of another age of uncertainty: apparent functionalism yet actual meaningless decoration, exaggeration of scale, the high tensions of melodrama. This was a style at once classical and anti-classical. The

127

★137   EUGENIO CARMI *Safety Sign* 1968 ▶

138   MARCELLO NIZZOLI *Olivetti* 1950 ▶

i piedi!

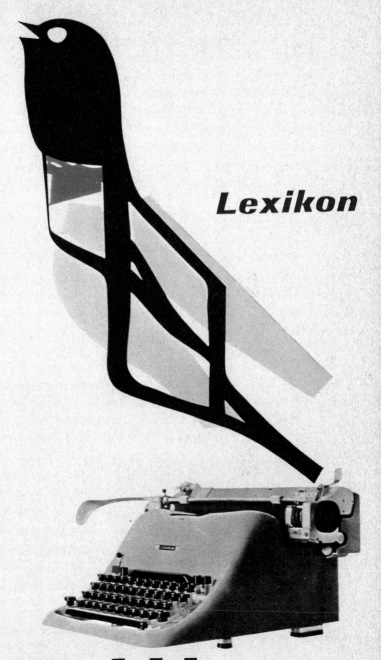

Lexikon

olivetti

new mannerism of the forties and fifties generally produced striking points of similarity. The earlier age had always suggested a world of movement and drama that seemed to anticipate the future art of the cinema; in the post-war years of the forties the cinema had come into its own. Films such as *Citizen Kane* by Orson Welles contained many of the devices of the mannerist tradition. Film techniques had already influenced poster design in the twentieth century, as in the work of Moholy-Nagy and El Lissitzky, but now the cinema was to exert an even greater influence on the appearance of posters. For example, 134 *German State Railways* (1955), by Eugene Max Cordier, demonstrates the mannerist devices of the period. First, ambiguity: the image is both descriptive and stylized, abstract and realistic – without too much of either. The underlying idea is to show how the passengers of a train (modernized to seem like air-travel) are presented with a picture-window view of the passing landscape. The outline of this window is also the shape of a cinema or television screen, implying that our vision is now conditioned by the viewfinder of the camera. Many posters have used this device of the outlined screen to enclose a visual quotation or simply to give an otherwise straightforward image the technical modernism of the photographic frame. In any case, film and television advertising forced the poster into a less significant role in visual advertising – at least as far as the development of new imagery was concerned.

139 HERBERT LEUPIN *Poster for a Printer in Lausanne* 1959

140 TOM ECKERSLEY Poster for General Post Office 1952

Eugene Max Cordier's poster has the double meaning of the two passengers being given the reality promised by the travelogue movie; further camera devices, such as close-up, the zoom and the effect of a panning shot, were all introduced into poster design. Among the important influences that contributed to the 'contemporary' style of posters were the Cubists' collage and textural effects, and other of their stylistic elements, such as the full-face profile image often used by Picasso and Braque in their paintings and drawings in the 1930s. Interpretations of the style of the School of Paris had already been given currency in posters through the work of Cassandre and others; now many designers made renewed use of these conventions. In Switzerland Herbert Leupin – *Poster for a Printer in Lausanne* (1959) – and Hans Erni produced elegant examples of this style; in France Raymond Savignac continued to make his sophisticated designs, for example, *Ma Colle*. In England, Tom Eckersley – *General Post Office* (1952) – and F. H. K. Henrion produced many designs that demonstrated the use of the simple, direct message of posters.

139

226, 140
136

131

Kieler Woche

21.-28. Juni 196

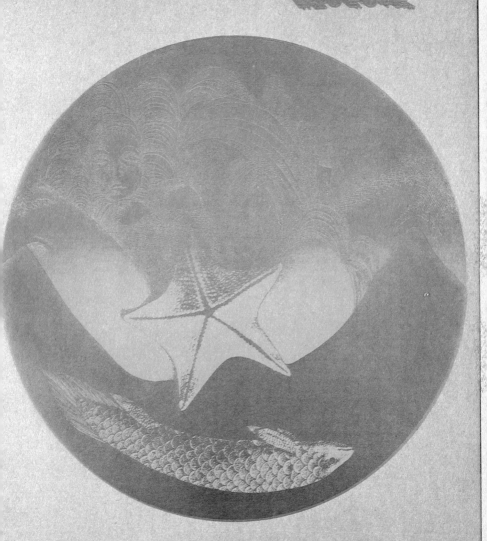

"静かの海,,の恐怖

悪こそ人間存在の本質である　　静かの海の深淵にひそむ暗黒にメスを入れ、現代の十字架の意味を問う伊藤ミカのオリジナル！

'09.8月〜10月　各金曜日　PM9.00〜11.00　赤坂スペースカプセル　伊藤ミカ.ビザール バレエ グループ（スペース カプセル ショウ）

STAFF　構成.演出／伊藤ミカ　音楽／一城蘭　照明／大田政志　美術／カガ現代美術会　コスチューム・デザイン／伊藤ミカ　コスチューム・製作（羽根・金属）／やまもと京子　コスチューム・毛／森　利広　宣伝美術／宇野亜喜良　制作／伊藤文学　DANCER　伊藤ミカ　青木信　川口緋

グループ事務所／文京区丈代2-11　Tel 421-5442　——　スペース・カプセル／港区赤坂3-15-13　Tel 585-0246-1　テーブル料￥500　ご飲食料￥400より　サービス料10%　税金10%

The main characteristic of the period after the Second World War was a rather uneasy attempt to make a connection with the posters of the thirties. This earlier and relatively 'innocent' era – the spirit of which was often reflected in the popular movies of the period as well as in advertising – could not compare with the complex nature of the Nuclear Age. In the 1960s, poster design, often produced by highly professional artists, became subject to influences that were more characteristic of a period of uncertainty, and took the form of a more emotional and erotic approach to visual advertising – for example, the 'sick' element of surrealist humour.

143 JAN LEWITT and GEORGE HIM *Post Office Lines of Communication* 1950

POST OFFICE LINES OF COMMUNICATION

CHAPTER THREE

Posters and Reality

EXPRESSIONISM

'I fear there is something essentially vulgar about the idea of the poster, unless it is limited to simple announcements of directions or becomes a species of heraldry or sign painting – the very fact of shouting loud, the association with vulgar commercial puffing, are against the artist and just so much dead weight.' These words by Walter Crane express a superior attitude towards the applied arts, as though the fine arts could never really function in the market place. However, one of the principal art movements, already gaining momentum in the late nineteenth century, was to raise the level of painting to a shout. This was the movement known as Expressionism, a forceful and emotional statement in the arts, which formed an alternative to the naturalism of much nineteenth-century work. Its origins can be traced in most non-Mediterranean countries and its roots extend back many centuries. With the paintings of Van Gogh and Edvard Munch, this form of expression was given currency: an example of particular significance is the design that Munch made in 1895 – *The Cry*. Munch had spent some years in Paris in the 1890s and we may assume that the posters of Toulouse-Lautrec and others had affected his art. But the establishment of Expressionist methods of strong emotional forms and bright colours was to become a significant influence on posters. For example, Jan Lenica's design for *Wozzeck* in 1964 is descended directly from Munch's earlier design. The use of Expressionist techniques in advertising raised the shout (from which Walter Crane had recoiled) to a scream. 235

In 1917 the use of Expressionist techniques, on one hand, and the purely realist treatment of subject-matter in advertising, on the other, became an issue when Roland Holst and Albert Hahn took part in a public discussion. In the introduction to an exhibition of 'Art in Advertising' in that year at the Stedelijk Museum in Amsterdam,

144   HENDRIK CASSIERS *Red Star Line c.* 1914

145   JO STEINER *Bier: Cabaret* 1919

146   G. M. MATALONI
Bec-Auer Gas Mantles 1895 ▶

Roland Holst wrote that poster artists now had the rare opportunity to serve a practical end at the same time as satisfying the need to produce something decorative as purely and as beautifully as possible, as well as meeting the demands of graphic art. He wrote:

> For nothing can be more eye-catching at present, amid the aimless characterlessness surrounding us, than something which has a firm purpose. It is both a waste of time and senseless to try and beat this lack of character at its own game, and at no time was it ever degrading to acknowledge oneself weaker than what is despicable.

Following an attack from the trade paper *De Bedrijfsreclame*, Roland Holst published his answer, which continued his argument, in

147 KARPELLUS
Koh-i-Noor

Over kunst en kunstenaars I (Amsterdam 1923). Included in this were these words:

> . . . . there are two things an advertisement can be. It can either be a simple piece of information or it can be a shout. . . . There is no need to shout out the truth, because it can be stated quietly without having to be over-emphasized.

The opposing view was presented by Albert Hahn in *Schoonheid en Samenleving* (Amsterdam 1929):

> What we are concerned with in art in advertising is a type of art seen by everybody, and one whose very nature enables it to influence even those people who care little for art and who, as a rule, would never consider entering an art gallery or an exhibition. It is street art pure and simple, and as such out and out popular.

Later, in another article which appeared in the journal of the Social Democratic Workers Party (*De Socialistische Gids*) he states:

> We live, unfortunately, in capitalistic circumstances still, our world is one of competition. Under the social conditions in which we live things are not produced in order to satisfy human needs, but, on the contrary, in a manner that is utterly anarchistic. . . . Why not a shout, if that is what is needed? If the artist is a genuine one, even his shouting is beautiful. . . . According to what he is asked to do . . . the artist will 'shout' or make his point emphatically in some other way. In doing so he will usually make use of strongly contrasting colours and simple shapes, since these make the most immediate appeal.

Though Hahn agreed with Roland Holst's views on purity of craftsmanship, he thought that the latest graphic techniques should be used to produce the clear and simple results that good advertising required. While praising Roland Holst's posters, he felt there were other ways of working, that instead of information and the requirements of lithography one could have the shout – in bold colours and simple forms. Although this exchange originally referred to posters in the Netherlands, the two attitudes are fundamental.

139

SOMMERAUSSTELLUNG
KÜNSTLER-
1921
VEREINIGUNG DRESDEN
JUNI   SEPT.
GEÖFFNET   SONNTAGS-10-6
WERKTAGS-9-7

Druck v.Oscar Laube, Dresden

149   ERNST LUDWIG KIRCHNER *Die Brücke* 1910

The poster that Ernst Ludwig Kirchner produced in 1910 for
149 the German art movement called *Die Brücke*, is a characteristic
example of Expressionism in poster form. Passionately nationalistic,
the poster is painted in the colours of the German Imperial flag. The
work is a striking alternative to the influence of Paris. *Die Brücke* as
an art movement had much of the wild colour that appeared in the
contemporary movement in France – the *Fauves* – but in addition
the members of the German movement were really an association
of independent artists and their public. Their work also seemed to
have more social awareness than the French paintings, which were
more concerned with light, warmth and colour in a purely sensuous
way. The German painters provided the work, and their public, by
joining the *Die Brücke* association, could contribute financially.
This exchange required a system of advertising, and it is in this
connection that there exists a direct relationship between Expressionism and the poster.

In Paris certain decorative elements had contributed to the
genesis of the poster, both from the traditional French sources –
the paintings of the eighteenth century – and from popular circus

150 WASSILY KANDINSKY Poster for the New
Artists' Union exhibition 1909

151 OSKAR KOKOSCHKA *Der Sturm*

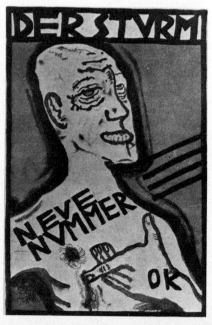

and fairground designs. Expressionism also had its sources, and these became new influences added to the growing stylistic background of poster art. These sources included the woodcuts and prints of the Middle Ages, as well as the work of more recent artists who, though they lived and worked in Paris, had explored new avenues: Vallotton (Swiss), Van Gogh and Van Dongen (Dutch), Munch (Norwegian). In addition, Gauguin's primitivism found a strong stylistic outlet through the work of the *Die Brücke* painters. Kirchner's poster is simple but also dramatic. This sense of drama – the drama of each individual – turns the poster into something much more dynamic than anything that Art Nouveau decoration could inspire.

Two aspects of Expressionism are distinguished by Paul Fechter in *Der Expressionismus* (1919): an intense Expressionism characterized by extreme individualism, and the experience of a painter like Pechstein 'whose creative impulse flows from a cosmic feeling which his will fashions and transforms'. The first type is exemplified by the work of Kandinsky, who, at the moment of most intense feeling, withdraws from the external world and achieves a visual transcendentalism with free forms and colours that are independent from the logic of appearances. The poster work of Kokoschka (*Der* *151* *Sturm* and the bathers of 1921) and Käthe Kollwitz belong to the second category.

In France, Henri Gustave Jossot's poster *Sales Gueules* (1899) and two posters by Steinlen show a similar use of pictorial drama that one associates with Expressionism: *Le Petit Sou* (1900) and a poster for his own work made in 1903. In the Netherlands an early example of this type of poster is found in the work of Mari Bauer (Marius Alex Jacques) in 1898. In Poland posters have often showed a markedly Expressionist character. In a poster for the Sztuka Association in 1898 Teodor Axentowicz produced a design that is an Expressionist version of Art Nouveau, strong and forceful – yet in the same year his contemporary Wojciech Weiss could produce a design for an artist's *soirée* that is a pale imitation of Parisian decoration.

The rise of Expressionism as a movement in the arts also coincided with the development of the cinema, and in Germany early films in

*152   ÉDOUARD DUYCK and ADOLPHE CRESPIN *Alcazar Royal – Bruxelles Sans-Gène*
1894

153 OTTO STAHL-ARPKE *The Cabinet of Dr Caligari* 1919

this style were remarkable examples of Expressionist art. Lotte Eisner has noted that 'the leaning towards violent contrast – which in Expressionist literature can be seen in the use of staccato sentences – and the inborn German liking for chiaroscuro and shadow, obviously found an ideal artistic outlet in the cinema.' These effects can easily be transcribed to posters, and the cinema poster in Germany certainly used Expressionist devices – for example, a work by Stahl-Arpke for *The Cabinet of Dr Caligari* (1919). In cases of this sort the film material was conceived in the same idiom. The elements of Expressionism that appear in Fritz Lang's *Metropolis* are echoed in the poster by Schulz-Neudamm advertising the film (1926). In England, Will Dyson designed a similarly dramatic poster for the film *Moriarty*.

153

More recently Expressionism has found its exponents in Roman
154 Cieślewicz – for example, his poster for Kafka's *The Trial* (1964) –
189 and Waldemar Swierzy, whose posters have strong colours edged in
heavy black outline. This technique of underlining the drawing
forcefully was given an ultimate expression in the poster by Jefim
155 Cwik of the Soviet Union, *May Day* (1965). An uncompromising
close-up of a clenched fist in thick, dark outline, it typifies the basic
element of force that the Expressionist image can produce. In this
case one is uncomfortably close to those monolithic images of power
that many regimes have used in their displays of propaganda.

Technical Expressionist devices, such as the distorted gesture or
the thick brush-mark and impasto, have also left their mark on
posters. Technique became the subject of much Abstract Expressionist painting in the United States and elsewhere. In 'action
paintings' – together with works described in France as Tachiste –
artists such as Georges Mathieu could adapt a painterly style to poster
design (*Air France*). The same company also used the rapid gestural

154 ROMAN CIEŚLEWICZ
The Trial 1964

155 JEFIM CWIK *May Day* 1965

mark of the loaded brush, implying speed, in a poster by Roger Excoffon in 1964. Such is the versatility of applied Expressionism that Excoffon was able to use the same technique for the Bally Shoe Company in 1965 – this time the sweeping curve of the artist's brush implied 'elegance'. In Switzerland Hans Falk has developed a series of painterly, decorative compositions, in which he makes use of brilliant slabs of colour that remind one of paintings by de Staël or de Kooning. The painterly use of broad areas of paint, as in Abstract Expressionism, has become part of the striking power of poster language: a number of posters submitted by leading designers for the Olympic Games of 1972 in Munich still use the language of Abstract Expressionism.

REALISM

In June 1919, speaking at an exhibition of Art in Advertising in Rotterdam, the designer Jac Jongert said: 'Power in advertising,

147

achievable through purity of design, can also be attained simply by reproducing the article itself clearly and beautifully, when it becomes as it were an advertising agent for the manufacturers.' Many critics, however, have felt that the poster sinks to the level of a catalogue illustration when the product as such is merely reproduced, and that instead poster art should be an exercise in sophisticated combinations of word and image. In fact, artists from Léger to Andy Warhol have used the advertiser's method of presenting an isolated object which, as a single image, has become part of visual experience. There are other reasons why this re-presentation of a product has been used so extensively. The meticulous representation of an object for sale, perhaps on a different scale from that of the original, helps to make that product a familiar part of one's experience and therefore easily recognizable in a shop. In any case a faithful reproduction, itself a quality product, helps to project confidence in the original.

The direct illustration in posters is as old as the poster itself. In fact, as we have seen, book illustration was one of the formative

156 H. N. WERKMAN Poster for a lecture on modern art 1920

157 HEMELMAN *Northern Cruises* 1926

158 EITAKU KANO
Herbal Pharmacy 1897

influences on the original development of pictorial advertising, which, when extended, becomes the poster as we know it. The way in which Chéret and others then established the combination of word and image gave the poster its special character, but nevertheless, the designer often reverted to the former practice of 'illustrating' the subject of the advertisement. By this time techniques in printing and the established language of poster-scale designs prevented the realistic poster from becoming confused with the advertisement on the page. Even Chéret himself produced designs of a descriptive kind, such as *Charité-Secours Familles Marina Naufragés* (1893). Moreau-Nélaton worked in this style, and the tradition was continued in the posters of Léon and Alfred Choubrac, such as *Lavabos*, *180* and in the delicate lithographs of Ibels – e.g., *L'Escarmouche* (1893). Eitaku Kano's poster *Herbal Pharmacy* (1897) in Japan shows a very *158* objective design from a country whose descriptions of 'the passing show' of the street are usually associated with stylization. Many of the entertainment posters of the *fin de siècle* used a straightforward descriptive method of displaying actresses and dancers as early examples of pin-ups: examples of this are the posters by Jules Alexandre Grün in Paris, such as *La Boîte à Fursy* (1899), which includes about twenty portrait heads, *La Cigale Générale* (1899) and *Les Petits Croisés* (1900). A similar combination of portraiture with the stylization of Art Nouveau appears in a poster by Duyck and Crespin (1894) in Brussels, *Alcazar Royal*. In Germany early examples of realistic designs are those of George Braumüller, *Amelang'sche Kunsthandlung* (1903); and Edmund Edel, *Berliner Morgenpost* (1902) and *Berliner Volks-Zeitung* (1909).

Many English posters for commercial products as well as those for entertainments were carried out in naturalistic terms – a common practice in most countries. Even pantomime posters in Great Britain, which might well have used the element of fantasy, as in the more rococo designs from France, were often illustrative in a realistic manner. In Amsterdam in 1890 a tea merchant, E. Brandsma,

159 BURKH–MONGOLD
Federal Swiss Song Festival Zürich 1905

160 BART VAN DER LECK *Rotterdam–London* 1919

organized a competition for an advertising card. Although the professional artistic jury selected finalists with suitable designs in the manner of fashionable Oriental patterns, he decided to award a special prize for the most suitable advertisement. The winning design was of an Oriental setting but conceived in a completely realistic Western manner.

The craze for cycling produced a number of cycling posters; even 221 Forain in 1891 and Toulouse-Lautrec in 1897 (*La Chaîne Simpson*) produced posters of the new machine. Pal (Jean de Paléologue), Misti (Misti-Mifliez), De Beers, Clouet, Busset, Chapellier and the Choubracs were other artists who made posters showing men, and 174 particularly women, perched high on the upright machines. These posters give an accurate account of the fashions of the period.

Another subject that attracted a realistic interpretation was sea-travel. In the Netherlands, posters such as *Red Star Line* (*c.* 1914) by 144 Cassiers or those by Van der Leck are examples of clear, illustrative 160 works in a technique that has been revived many times in every country. This toy-like world has a universal appeal and, because of its commonplace vision, can be understood at a glance. These posters, however, invite close inspection and belong to the tradition of coloured prints of ships.

Posters that illustrated with precision the new mechanical resources of the twentieth century were only one area of realistic design. Realism was employed to advertise high-quality products generally, for the careful craft of engraving could convey an accurate picture. The skilled work of artists in black and white, such as that of Frank Brangwyn (1867–1956) in England still maintained standards of representation that the camera could not equal. At the end of the First World War, however, the work of photographers such as Arnold Genthe (1869–1942) could compete with the hand-made image, and photography became acceptable in posters. This was developed in the United States in particular, where most advertising in any case became naturalistic in presentation. Commercial enterprises in this quickly developing society made use of realistic painting

161, 162 GAN HOSOYA In these posters for Sapporo Breweries the sharply focused detail, intended to stimulate thirst, is also given an element of fantasy by the use of montage 1968

"The heart has its own reasons"   Pascal

School of Visual Arts   209-213 East 23 Street, New York 10, N. Y.   MUrray Hill 3-8397

163   GEORGE TSCHERNY Poster for School of Visual Arts, New York 1961

164 J. C. LYENDECKER *Chesterfield Cigarettes* 1926

for the page and the billboard. Following the decorative art-posters in the style of Art Nouveau, posters in the United States were more directly attached to the demands of commerce, which, even in Europe (as we have seen), would have became more realistic if left to the decisions of businessmen. In the United States, the decorative arts of Paris or movements like De Stijl and Constructivism were not close enough geographically or artistically to provide sufficient influence. Instead a realistic image, although this might take a humorous form, was more generally acceptable. By 1941 this process had even succeeded in minimizing the effects of the European styles that had appeared in the United States in the late thirties. In the New York Art Directors' 23rd Annual Report (1941) one finds this statement:

> The flat 'European' poster technique has been more and more discarded in favour of a three-dimensional rendering. Color photography, photomontage and the airbrush have helped to streamline the American poster. . . . Realistic-naturalistic posters are by far in the majority, with only an occasional modern, abstract or symbolic design here or there.

But this represented the supremacy of a trend in poster design that

154

had been a continuous development. In 1924 it is found in Lyendecker's poster, *The Dancing Couple*. There are several variations of his design but always painted in careful detail. The calculated response to such faithful realism is similar to the feelings evoked by John Ruskin in his description of Holman Hunt's painting, *The Awakening Conscience*, which was printed in *The Times* in May 1854. Ruskin described the effect of the painstaking realism of all the subsidiary details; in Lyendecker's poster it is, for example, the simple, freshly pressed party clothes of the couple that produce a sentimental response. The large billboard gave a new dimension to this portrayal *164* of naturalism, and designers such as Ruzzie Green, Howard Scott, Lester Beall, Paul Rand and Jack Welch all provided designs of impeccable accuracy. Their work reflected a popular concept of the consumer society, illustrated in Welch's *Drake's Cookies* (1956), which used humour as well as photographic realism. A small boy who has been attacked by a greedy colleague is shown still happily in possession of his cookie. The biscuit and every freckle on his face are presented with clinical accuracy. Artists such as Hohlwein from Germany had also contributed to this tradition of realistic art in commercial advertising, but the real influence had been the small

165 ATELIER YVA, BERLIN *Jelsbach & Co. c.* 1927

166 YUSAKA KAMEKURA *Kokudo Keikaku Co. Ltd* 1968

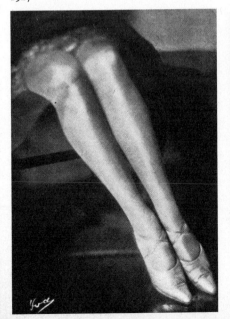

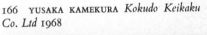

photographic, magazine advertisement – a glossy, realistic picture which was enlarged to billboard proportions. This represented the perfect image of the ideal world of the successful citizen – a world that one could buy and an environment that advertising was helping to create.

In Europe the effects of photography on poster design also came from the same sources as the other *avant-garde* influences. Artists like Lissitzky and Moholy-Nagy expressed their ideas not only in paint but also with a camera. Photography and typography were used together in the new developments pioneered by Piet Zwart and Jan Tschichold. In his book *Asymmetric Typography*, first published in 1935 and quoted here in Ruari McLean's first English translation in 1967, Tschichold writes, under the heading 'Typography, photography and drawings':

> The signs and letters in the composing room are not the only means at the disposal of the new typography. Pictures are often better than words; they convey more and say it quicker. The natural method of pictorial representation today is photography. Its uses are now so varied that we would be lost without them. The quality of the photograph is a decisive factor in the success of any job which uses it. Photography has its own rules, which are based on the same principles as those of the new typography.
>
> As well as normal photography, for example, photograms (photography without a camera, a technique developed and made new by Moholy-Nagy and Man Ray), negative photography, double exposures and other combinations (e.g. the outstanding self-portrait of Lissitzky) and photomontage. Any or all could be used in the service of graphic expression. They can help to make a message clearer, more attractive and visually richer. . . . Photography, drawing and type are all parts, to make up a whole. In their proper subordination to that whole lies the value of their use.

The work of Tschichold, one of the most significant single influences on design generally – including the poster – shows clearly how photography, as a design element, should be linked with other elements. Many posters, however, rely on the effect of a large photograph by itself. Although this can achieve a striking image it is really nothing more than a blow-up from the page of a magazine. In order to make the same product part of a billboard advertisement it is necessary to isolate an object – if necessary by representing it accurately, but achieving a new reality by the simple process of enlargement. 167

This leads us to consider the step that we now take beyond reality when a realistic image is isolated and enlarged. An element of fantasy is introduced at the sight of a perfectly normal image that has become a giant. The effect of fantasy is increased if the image is banal or if in some way the incongruity of the new situation is exploited. Sometimes an atmosphere of super-reality is created by the attempts of the advertisers to try to shout louder than their rivals, and it is this free-for-all that has produced some of the most exciting, indigenous material, which artists like Claes Oldenburg and Tom Wesselmann have used as raw material for their work. 213

A more sophisticated approach to the process of making quotations from the real world than the direct method of creating a

167 ANONYMOUS
Nelbarden Swimwear
1969

realistic image, was pioneered by Braque and Picasso in their Cubist experiments, and by Boccioni and his associates in the Futurist movement. Braque introduced designs of everyday lettering, such as the stencil and newsprint, into his compositions; Picasso made similar use of this actual quotation from reality and increased the possibilities of this departure by including three-dimensional objects – thus anticipating the art of assemblage. In his painting *The Cavalry Charge*, Boccioni shows how the introduction of a section of newsprint lends a feeling of immediate reportage; for all its modernity, the work would otherwise still remain a conventional easel painting.

Futurism, like Cubism, was based on reality, and had a direct effect on poster design through the experiments made in typography. 'I am against what is known as the harmony of a setting,' wrote Marinetti in 1909; 'when necessary we shall use three or four columns to a page and twenty different typefaces. We shall represent *hasty perceptions* in italics, and express a **Scream** in **Bold** type; a new painterly typographic representation will be born on the printed page.' A comparison between the use of lettering in Cubist and Futurist painting explains the nature of the different influences at work. In a Cubist painting the fragmentary quotations of words and letters like *Valse, Bar, Pernod, Rhum, Journal, Ma Jolie* are associations with the real world: one might call them drops of sentiment in the otherwise austere interpretation of reality that Cubism presented. The letters are always in Old Face capitals – a link with the classical world of the past. In Futurist lettering we find aggressive, phonetic symbols conveying a message, such as Basta Basta Basta, VOOOooooo, scrAbrrRaaNNG, SIMULTAN-EITA, ESPLOSIONE, using a variety of type. Although the Futurists used some of the devices of the Cubists, they were also borrowing the note of immediacy and sensationalism from political broadsheets. In fact, the mixed type used in the popular political and music-hall bills of the eighteenth and nineteenth centuries is the ancestor of this typographical variety.

Futurist art was concerned with restlessness and dynamism – qualities of great importance to advertising – and it was not, in any sense, a formal art movement. Nor was Dada – a movement quite

158

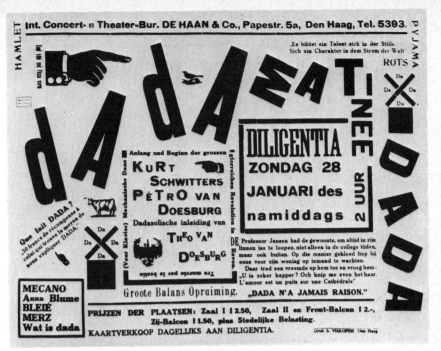

168   KURT SCHWITTERS and THEO VAN DOESBURG Poster for Dada recital in The Hague 1923

opposed to the Futurist love of war; the Dadaists registered despair at a war-mad mechanical world. Both movements used pictorial quotations of chaotic typography – the world of the popular advertisement. From this derivation the movements created new styles which, in turn, were absorbed back into poster design. The sensationalism of Kurt Schwitters' trash-images and much of the subject-matters of the photo-montages of John Heartfield derive from the street and the popular press. The giant poem conceived by Raoul Hausmann in 1919 found an echo in the work displayed in the magazine of calligraphic art, *Rhinozeros*, first published in Germany in 1960. In this journal the ideas and decorative possibilities of ornamental lettering were pushed much further than was possible in commercial advertising. It contained the work of Klaus-Peter and Rolf-Gunter Dienst, Ferdinand Kriwet and Frans Mon, all artist/poets who used the form-making properties of typography – sometimes in the poster-poem.

168

Roussillon

FRENCH RAILWAYS

169 SALVADOR DALI *Roussillon*
(French Railways) 1969

170 TETSUO MIYAHARA *Jazz St Germain* 1968

SURREALISM

The Dadaists' methods of juxtaposition and surprise – the shock derived from seeing an unlikely or unexpected association of realistic elements – were also used by the Surrealists. When André *170* Breton declared Dada dead in 1924 and proclaimed the arrival of Surrealism, he introduced a movement whose vitality is still apparent in the 1970s. Surrealism may be defined as the revelation of a new dimension of reality, made possible when the logic of reason is removed and an arbitrary association of images of the real world is substituted. This produces a fresh experience.

Freud once remarked to Salvador Dali that what interested him in Dali's paintings was the 'conscious' element and not the uncon- *169* scious. By this, one can assume, as Arnold Hauser has pointed out, he implied that he was interested, not in the simulated paranoia of Dali's work, but in the method of simulation. For Dali had reversed the process necessary for the 'production' or inducement of sur- realist manifestations – that is, to allow the unconscious mind to produce images illogically. It appears that he often searched the sub-conscious for imagery. The 'style' of his work has probably

161

accounted for the accusation that his work appears too commercialized and exhibitionist as a result. But whatever may have been said, the whole of Dali's work represents art based on realism related to the sur-realist world of dreams, and his method, which has provided him with an opportunity for some virtuoso performances in the visual arts has had an immense effect on advertising. Other painters in the movement, such as Magritte and Ernst, can of course claim a significant share in the contribution, but it is the work of Dali that captured the popular imagination. In any case he, like Duchamp, demonstrated his technical devices in window display, but Duchamp's work is necessarily obscure, and Dali's remains obvious.

Poster designers have made use of Surrealism for three very simple reasons. In the first place, the use of realism makes the work familiar and acceptable. Secondly, the shock of finding that the image is not what was first supposed acts as a forceful reminder of

*171   GRANDVILLE *Metamorphoses* 1854

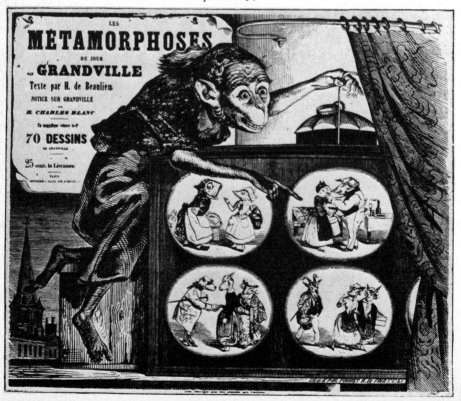

172 FERDINAND LUNEL *Rouxel and Dubois c.* 1896

that image. Thirdly, it is legitimate in Surrealist art to present an idea in several ways simultaneously. This can be done visually, without explanation or justification – an invaluable device for exhibiting a product and its effects in one design.

Of course, one can find examples of 'surrealism' before the movement was announced in the 1920s. The work of Arcimboldo in the sixteenth century, or the anthropomorphic fantasies of Grandville *171* in the nineteenth, or in the same period the popular postcards of Killenger, in which landscapes are built up out of human forms. In fact, popular art, including posters – for example, the one by Lunel for *Rouxel and Dubois* in the 1890s – provided source material for the *172* Surrealists of 1924. Many of the cycling posters and advertisements, such as Tamango's *Terrot* (1898) or the anonymous poster for the *173*

163

TERROT
DIJON
CYCLES
AUTOMOBILE
M. CHAPUIS
RUE BOSSUET
8
AFFICHAGE
TAMAGNO
T.C.F. SEULE MÉDAILLE D'OR

173   TAMANGO *Terrot*
Cycles and Automobiles
1898

174   CHOUBRAC *Humber*
Cycles c. 1896

Dangerfield and Co., reveal some of the tensions that existed between man and machine in the new age of technology. It was one of the achievements of the *avant-garde* to exploit the element of fantasy in naïve art, the poster of popular inspiration being a principal source of raw material – for example, Alfred Jarry and the celestial cyclists of his saga, *The Passion Considered as an Uphill Bicycle Race*. In fact, in 1924 the designer D'Ylen was using imagery closely related to that of Surrealism in his posters for the Shell Company.

179

The influence of Surrealism on posters may be seen in two distinct phases. The first lasted from the 1920s until the end of the Second World War. The second starts in the 1950s and is still alive in the '70s. The first phase represents a close, direct quotation from the Surrealist movement but its translation into advertising is on the level of decoration – especially in terms of the theatre. During the second phase, after the terrible revelations of the war that ended in

175   SKAWONIUS Swedish theatre poster *c.* 1938

1945 and the uneasy peace that has followed, it is the more sinister and horrific imagery released by the Surrealist painters that has gained general expression through advertising.

There are exceptions to this rather obvious interpretation, such as the frightening imagery of John Heartfield from the earlier phase, and the lyrical Surrealism of Push Pin Studios, in the '60s, which is reminiscent of the more decorative innocence in the '30s. But these exceptions merely underline the fact that Surrealism itself contained both the macabre visions of Max Ernst and the apparent tranquility of Paul Delvaux's moonlit landscapes. In fact, since our society has become outspoken about its state of unrest the condition of uneasiness is relieved by making public use of vicious and violent imagery in advertising as well as in most of the mass media generally. In any case, advertising can hardly lag behind the material on display in the cinema and on television. In the first phase – that is, until the end of the Second World War – poster designers borrowed elements of Surrealist composition, such as the dramatic lighting and long, cast shadows of De Chirico and Dali. This can be seen in the poster 176 *Ambre Solaire* by Cassandre. The props of the 'metaphysical' paintings of De Chirico and Morandi appear, for example, in a poster

176 T. MORALIS *Greece*
1952

177   GEORGE HIM *The Times* 1952

from the thirties by Mahler for men's clothing. Some of the most
unusual works are the three-dimensional 'surrealist' assemblages of
270–273 Gumitsch in the same period. In this respect they recall the work of
Dali for Bonwit Teller's store in New York and his exhibition
works, such as *Rainy Taxi*; they also remind one of the close links
between advertising and the world of Surrealism at that time.

The theatre attracted the talents of Cocteau, on one hand, and
Cassandre, on the other. Theatrical elements, such as the quotation
175 of the carefully rolled cloud, or the single draped curtain, became
acceptable symbols of 'exterior' or 'interior', so that a blank stage
or an advertisement layout might contain one of these elements and
that would be sufficient to set the right atmosphere. A further
element was taken from pre-war Surrealism – the use of humour
and the absurd. This was used in the designs of Savignac and, in the
second phase of Surrealist advertising, in the work of George
177 Him – *The Times* (1952). This language of Surrealist symbolism
has remained with the poster ever since. One of the most subtle
interpretations of Surrealist techniques can be seen in Herbert
178 Matter's *All Roads Lead to Switzerland* (1935) – this appears to be a

168

178   HERBERT MATTER *All Roads Lead to Switzerland* 1935 ▶

All roads lead to

SWITZERLAND

SHELL

FOR THE UTMOST
HORSE POWER

180   A. CHOUBRAC *Lavabos*

◀ 179   JEAN D'YLEN *Shell* 1924

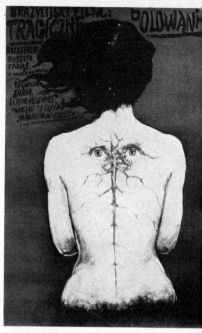

181 JOHN HEARTFIELD (HELMUT HERZFELD)
For the Crisis Party Convention of the S.P.D.
(photomontage) 1931

182 FRANCISZEK STAROWIEYSKI Brazilian
poster 1969

photograph of mountain landscape, but in fact it is a montage of
various naturalistic photographs, which, when assembled, convey a
new reality that is strangely unreal.

    The photo-montage works of John Heartfield, which anticipated
the tragic horrors of persecution and total war, made use of the
combined devices of Dada and Surrealism to present posters of great

181   political force: for example, *For the Crisis Party Convention of the
S.P.D.* (1931). Heartfield's work, which seemed at the time to be
the exception, has now been followed by a generation of poster designers whose work resembles his. Heinz Edelmann, in his poster for

227   a film by Buñuel, Klaus Warwas and Starowieyski have all produced savage imagery which is accepted by a hardened society.

183   Bizarre and erotic elements are used in posters such as *Chelsea Girls*
by Alan Aldridge, and in those by Martin Sharp and Michael
English, although the Surrealist influence is often deliberately confused with other stylistic elements. The more erotic Surrealist

183   ALAN ALDRIDGE Film poster for Andy Warhol's *Chelsea Girls* 1968 ▶

184   MILTON GLASER (Push Pin Studios) *From Poppy with Love* 1967 (Overleaf)

185   PETER MAX *Outer Space* 1967 (Overleaf)

for the first time in this country in
its original continuous version running
for 3½ hours on two screens uncut

Andy Warhol's

Chelsea Girls

Oct 16th-19th (Wed-Sat) 23rd-26th (Wed-Sat)
7.00 pm till 12.00 midnight tickets 10/- (Bookable) 7/6
Arts Laboratory 182 Drury Lane WC2. 242-3407/8

peter max

186　PIETER
BRATTINGA
Carnaval 1958

187 TEISSIG Poster
for French
film 1966

imagery used in advertising in the 1970s makes the posters of the
pre-war years seem innocent and discreet by comparison. In Poland,
besides the work of Starowieyski and Cieślewicz, that of Lenica   *182, 154*
demonstrates that the unrest revealed in the visions of the twenties
and thirties has become the generally accepted language of the
period of uncertainty following the Second World War. The work
of Tomi Ungerer also reflects a 'sick' society and is connected with
that of Saul Steinberg, who was one of the first artists to re-interpret
the Surrealist language in terms of the post-war society. The use of   *184*
Surrealism in these terms is universal, from Push Pin Studios and
Peter Max in the United States to Tadanori Yokoo and Shigeru   *188*
Miwa in Japan, from Armando Paeltorres in the Argentine to   *191*
Brattinga in Holland and Teissig in Czechoslovakia.   *187*

177

188   TADANORI YOKOO *Laboratory of Play* c. 1968 ▶
189   WALDEMAR SWIERZY Polish travel poster 1969 ▶

SPEND YOUR HOLIDAYS IN **POLAND**

n Mazury, the land of ten thousand lakes

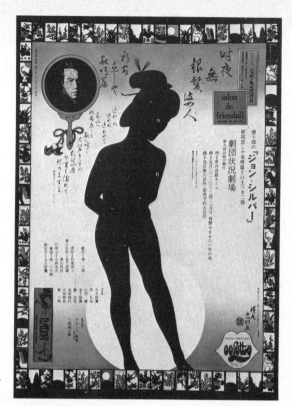

190 TADANORI YOKOO Theatre poster
c. 1968

191 SHIGERU MIWA Poster advertising a collection of modern American short stories c. 1968

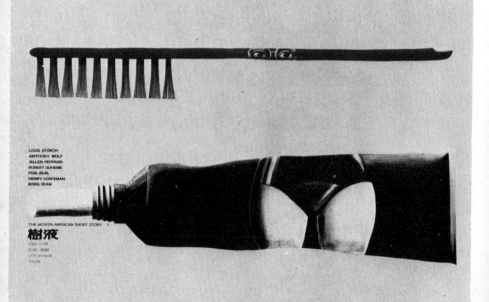

On the poster:

An Alan Clore Films pro...
WONDERWALL...
starring
JACK MacGOWRAN · JANE BIRKIN
guest starring
IRENE HANDL · RICHARD WATTIS and Iain Quarrier
Screenplay...
From an original story by G...
...GEORGE HARRISON M...
...
POOR OSCAR,
HE ONLY
WANTED TO
WATCH HER
THROUGH THE
WONDERWALL

192   HARRY GORDON *Wonderwall* 1969

'A mere collection of dreams without the dreamer's associations, without the knowledge of the circumstances in which they occurred, tells me nothing and I can hardly imagine what it could tell anyone': so Freud wrote to André Breton. For diagnosis such detached evidence is perhaps meaningless, but as a method, as a convention in the visual arts, it has provided some powerful ideas in the history of art in general and of poster design.

BLACKPOOL

*193   JOHN HASSALL *Blackpool c.* 1912

CHAPTER FOUR

Posters and Society

THE POPULAR IDIOM

A poster can never be obscure. The designer cannot allow his work to express a private idea that subsequent generations may be able to unravel: he must achieve instant contact. To do this he must, like an entertainer, work with his audience. In many cases it becomes necessary to speak to the unprofessional audience in a popular way, although there are also times when an audience expects a degree of technical brilliance. Posters frequently reflect the popular idiom because their function is to communicate as well as to be decorative. Because visual communication is the first justification for their existence, it is the character and extent of popular influence on their appearance that establishes the peculiar nature of posters as such. In fact, it is in this area of expression that one finds the essential qualities of the poster as opposed to its near relations, the painting or the graphic image. Because of the technical problems of design – in actual printmaking as well as in the sphere of aesthetics – the appearance of posters is mainly governed by professional artistic factors: that is to say, fashions in style and means of expression. Some of these we have examined – Art Nouveau, Constructivism, Surrealism. It is often thought that posters are necessarily a compromise of artistic styles, but we have seen that they frequently express visual ideas as well as paintings have done. In fact, posters have sometimes affected the other arts. When this reciprocal process has occurred, it is precisely the popular aspect of poster design that has caught the imagination of painters, for it is the expression of the popular idiom that gives the poster its unique place in the arts.

The popular idiom has two main directional currents. One flows upwards from the level of folk art and brings with it a common factor of integrity and a certain naïvety. The other current flows downwards and is usually called mass culture; it is commercial or political propaganda, generally pre-digested and made palatable for mass-consumption. The dangerous aspect of this situation is that one current comes to seem like the other. In other words, the doctrinaire approach of the poster of the totalitarian state, which presents an image of satisfied, cooperative citizens and subjects (no less false than the exactly equivalent poster of the free consumer society, which presents material gains as a doctrinaire aspect of another type of regime), is made to seem a true reflection of the popular condition. It is not a reflection in either case, but a projection from the forces in power.

196 An example of a poster in the folk-art tradition is the design made by Fraipont at the turn of the century for the French town of Royat. It has the form of the cover of a provincial brochure or the decorative label of a cheese-box. Many of the posters made at this time for household products presented a world in which the consumer could recognize himself. It did not take long, however, for the advertiser to discover that he could project a more luxurious world which could be attained by the consumer if he bought the product. The effect of the poster that displayed the rewards of the acquisitive consumer society was summed up in the statement by President Sukarno of Indonesia that refrigerators are a symbol of revolution – to a community that does not possess them.

But whatever the nature of its sources, the poster in the popular idiom speaks the language of the mass of spectators – whether it contains the naïvety of folk art or the pretentiousness of *Kitsch*. The popular poster seems to have proceeded from one situation

194   THOMAS THEODOR HEINE *Gustav Schiebel and Company*

LA TERRIBLE NOCHE
Del 17 de Agosto de 1890.
ltimos recuerdos del Sargento 2° Zeferino Martínez

195   JOSE GUADALUPE POSADA *La Terrible Noche* 1890

towards the other, and we can begin to examine its history
with the earliest pictorial designs, such as the nineteenth-century
gallows literature, consisting of popular melodramatic material,
which has its counterpart in lively circus, fairground and bullfight
advertising. The popular designs of nineteenth-century broadsheets
concerning the escapades of criminals have a stylistic parallel in the
misadventures illustrated in the votive primitives of churches in
Italy at the same time. All these startling images were brought
together in the remarkable graphic work of José Guadalupe Posada
(1851–1913), who added to the dramatic character of the genre the
forceful imagery of Mexican art. This fierce, primitive quality is
shown in *La Terrible Noche*. The history of bullfighting posters is a   195

185

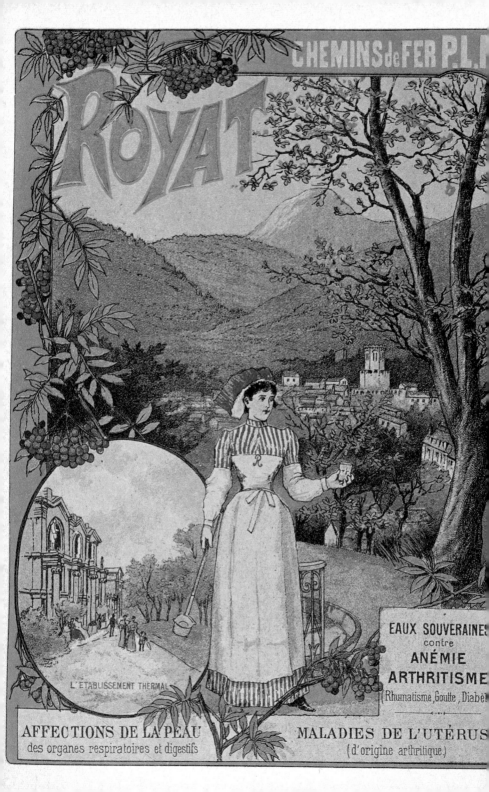

long one, and, as a source of inspiration for the poster, comparable to the circus and fairground designs from which Chéret derived part of his own experience. One of the most original is the circular 199 design of *Cartel en Circulo de Madrid*: one of the most splendid 200 examples is dated 1906, richly coloured in gold. Most of these examples of folk art have great professional artistic merit. In order to find posters that have the awkward quality of a popular attempt to create complicated allegories and elaborate compositions, it is necessary to look at the efforts of the printing establishments, such 198 as Dangerfield and Co. in London in the 1890s.

Some of the designs of Dudley Hardy in England, such as his poster for *St. Paul's Magazine*, and of John Hassall in *When Knights Were Bold* (1900), *A Greek Slave* (1900) and *Amaris* (1900), all have this same quality, although both these artists could sometimes produce more professional works with greater unity and assurance. In France, where, judging by contemporary critical accounts, there was a higher standard of poster work, the popular idiom was conveyed by painters capable of producing posters that did not strain after style but expressed an easy, natural descriptive manner. Work 201 such as that of Anquetin and Vallotton, of 'Pal' in *Cabourg* or Metivet in *Eugénie Buffet* (1893), demonstrates this. Many of the posters of Steinlen, as we have seen already in connection with his 'social' realism, were exceptional designs with a strong popular appeal. In Germany this type of poster was interpreted in designs of a more rounded, decorative kind, such as the posters by Ortmann:

198 ANONYMOUS Theatre poster composed and printed by Dangerfield & Co. *c.* 1896

199 ANONYMOUS *Cartel en Circulo de Madrid* 1856

CABOURG
5 hs DE PARIS.
GRAND-HOTEL
RESTAURANT
CAFE
DIRECTION
H. NOËL & PATTARD.
CASINO.
THEATRE.
CONCERTS.
BALS.
PAL
LA PLUS BELLE PLAGE
IMPRIMERIE-PAUL·DUPONT: 4, RUE DE BOULOI · PARIS·

Heize mit Gas (1912) and *Odeon* of the same year. A work by the
Czech, Ottokar Stafl (*Baška*), as well as the posters of the Belgian
designers who worked in a realistic idiom, such as Evenpoel,
Rassenfosse, Duyck and Crespin, or the Dutch designer Cassiers,
whose posters have the same general appeal, show that the anecdotal
nature of popular designs could be interpreted by artists of real
ability. It also indicates the fact that popular art is always conceived
in terms of realism.

A straightforward, objective design will always have a general appeal and the clumsy, amateur design will always find acceptance with
the public. These two elements are constant factors when one con-
siders the nature of the popular idiom in poster design. After the
First World War, the public had become conditioned to accept many
of the more sophisticated discoveries of professional artists who had
made a contribution to the appearance of posters in the streets. The
designs of James Pryde and William Nicholson, for example, which
had at the turn of the century represented the exception in good

229

202 J. G. VAN CASPEL *Amsterdam Printer* 1905

203 CHOBSOR Poster for air display 1910

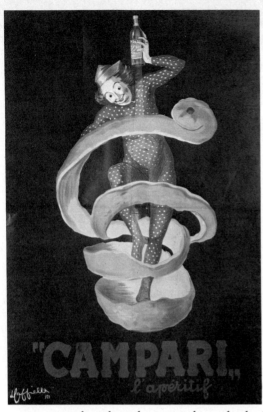

204 LEONETTO CAPPIELLO *Campari, l'Apéritif* 1921

poster art rather than the general standard of most hoardings, now became more generally acceptable. The convention of simplicity that they and great designers such as Toulouse-Lautrec had established now became part of what most people regarded as poster technique. Posters by Frank Newbould, Tom Purvis and Gregory Brown in England gave the experiments of the 'Beggarstaff Brothers' popular currency. But the development of the simple, economic statement had other justifications. The poster of the 1920s had to appeal to motorists as well as the more leisurely passer-by in the street. By 1956 a writer on advertising from the United States, H. W. Hepner, could say that in designing a poster 'one should assume that the people who see it cannot or at least will not read it. It must tell its whole story in about six seconds.' Leonetto Cappiello, who held a dominant position as a designer in France from the start of the century until the '20s, was, as we have seen, one of the first artists to appreciate this new

94

204

205–07 Three examples of outdoor advertising, showing how the poster designer's work assumes a new significance when the result is seen on the street. A street in Paris in the 1950s (*left*) contrasted with two views (*right*, and *opposite*) of streets in Germany taken 40 years earlier

factor. His posters, such as *Amandines de Provence* (1901), seemed to many critics at the time to be merely abbreviated versions of *fin-de-siècle* designs. In fact, his contribution to the development of the poster lies in the way he and other designers reduced the image to a single element – often exaggerated – that could be retained by the memory at a glance. The value of an instant judgment with respect to more serious works of art had already been expressed by Baudelaire, who had spoken of 'certain irrefutable truths suggested by a first rapid and generalized glance' when writing of a painting by Delacroix. The instant summing-up of swift movement was in any case one of Delacroix's achievements. Much of this visual shorthand, both as a method and as a mental discipline, passed into the art of the twentieth century although, like Chéret, Delacroix may appear to be one of the last of a line of Old Masters rather than the innovator that he was in reality.

In order to translate this rapid, telegraphic message into permanent visual form it was necessary to make flat patterns of very simple shape rather than linear notes. While the line is quicker to record, the flat pattern is easier to assimilate and its block-like form is literally imprinted on the mind like an after-image. As the poster moved into the 1920s and 1930s it retained its popular effects in this new shorthand. At the same time, the more conventional designs for posters

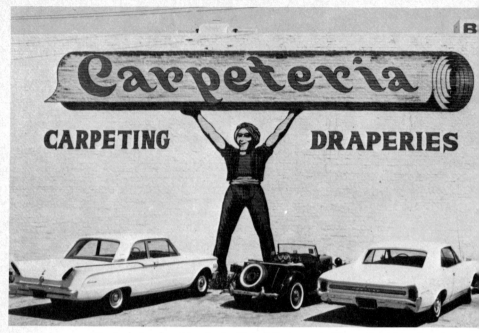

208 Scale in advertising in the United States 1968 (Photo: David Hockney)

74 continued – work such as that of Poulbot and Dransy in France. The development from the popular idiom that has had the greatest effect on poster design was derived from the growth in size of the actual design itself. This was most apparent in the billboard designs in the United States. Partly the result of the need to shout louder, but also to meet the same increase of speed that we have just discussed, the

208–210
212 American billboard established a new scale of image that was eventually imitated by the cinema in various developments of the wide screen. The designs that appeared on them were produced during the period when, as we have seen, the predominant style of poster as well as all pictorial advertising in the United States was realistic. These murals displayed giant girls in swim-wear, or plates of steaming beans alongside the highway network; they also obliterated the façades of city architecture, and established a form of urban

209   In the United States the extended billboard, which originally anticipated the wide cinema-screen . . .

210   . . . later imitated the moving frame 1968 (Photos: David Hockney)

decoration based entirely on the popular idiom. In the late 1960s two European film directors of distinction made films about the United States in which they showed long sequences of billboards. In *Midnight Cowboy*, John Schlesinger showed a startling image of urban New York, and in *Zabriskie Point* Michelangelo Antonioni presented, in clear-cut focus, the fresh colours and vivid presence of the art forms of the consumer society. The result of the incongruity of these images, although originally realistic in concept, has been to produce a new mythology and fantasy that painters have been quick to recognize as raw material for their own statements, and the popular billboard has been responsible for exerting an immense influence on the appearance of painting since 1945. At the same time, the original advertisements have come to be considered as desecrations of the landscape – Hawaii even banned their presence as early as 1927, Vermont since the beginning of 1970. The larger the billboard the greater the offence to sensitive planners, and the more compulsively fascinating the banal images become to many painters.

It becomes necessary, therefore, to examine the effect of the popular poster on painting and sculpture, in order to identify the exact nature of the popular idiom in the poster. As early as 1916–17 Marcel Duchamp adapted a Sapolin Enamel advertisement to read 'Apolinère Enameled'. The illustration showed a typically incongruous popular arrangement of a little girl wearing her best dress, painting her bed – a suitably ridiculous situation for Duchamp to parody. The popular poster for *Savon Cadum* (which was nicknamed Bébé Cadum) was often quoted by those who, in the early twenties, realized the comic possibilities of these solemn advertisements. It was used by Picabia and René Clair in their film *Entr'acte* in 1924 – one of the last manifestations of Dada – and was quoted by Cassandre in a description of Paris, gripped by advertising and illuminations, beneath the smiling baby and the glowing Eiffel Tower, in 1928. The Surrealists also made use of popular advertising, including that of posters. In 1936, in the exhibition of Surrealist art at the Museum of Modern Art in New York there appeared a design – *The Lawn Party of the Royal Worcester Corset Company* 1906 – which shows a crowd gathered below a flying corset. The same exhibition made use

211 ANONYMOUS *Shirley Temple* 1936

of the window-display techniques of draped dummies. All these
visions connect Surrealism with popular forms of advertising. Many
of the original advertisements were Surrealist images in their own
right – one needed merely to re-present them.

One of the most significant uses that an artist was to make of
the popular poster image is Duchamp's secret work *Etant Donnés . . .*,
prepared over a number of years from 1946 to 1966, and revealed
only after his death in 1968. In his youth Duchamp would have been
familiar with a series of popular posters advertising gas-mantles,
which were a similar genre to the many cycling posters that existed

212 Scale in advertising in the United States 1967. (Photo: David Hockney)

in the early 1900s. In most cases the *Bec-Auer* posters showed a semi-naked girl holding a lighted gas-mantle. Examples of these posters include works such as that by Réalier-Dumas (1893) and Mataloni (1895). In the latter, a girl wearing a see-through slip, tucked under her bare breasts, holds a sunflower in one hand, while drawing attention to the glowing gas-mantle with the other. Around the border of the poster, the fashionable Art Nouveau tendrils of organic growth have been replaced by the complicated plumbing of the gas engineer. Faced with such formidable imagery, Duchamp prepared a tableau of this *Kitsch* image but took care that his finished work should be enshrined in an academic setting – the work can be seen only by peeping, voyeur-like, through two holes in a door in the Philadelphia

146

Museum, where most of his work rests. The creative artist has to be on his guard against the banality of the commonplace and the lifelessness of respectability. Duchamp went to both extremes by taking a banal poster image and placing it in the museum: in this way he finds a solution to the dilemma of the creative artist in the twentieth century. He adopts a third position and creates art out of an attitude. Léger found a different solution:

> In 1919 I painted a picture using only pure colour surfaces. The picture is technically a revolution. It was possible, without tone or modulation, to produce depth and dynamism. Advertising benefited first from the results. Pure colour, blues, reds, yellow, escaped from this painting into posters, shop windows, road signs and signals. Colour had become free, it was a reality in itself. It had a new life wholly independent of the object which before this period contained and supported it.

Léger was himself also to derive much from the exchange. His use of the single, isolated object was borrowed (as Christopher Green noted in his introductory essay to an exhibition of Léger's work at the Tate Gallery, London in 1970,) from typical advertising layout as displayed in *L'Illustration*.

In 1924 Stuart Davis made a painting which was untitled but represented an Odol toothpaste poster design. This did not present the sentimental popular image of the Bébé Cadum poster but the modern pack of the toothpaste container, and therefore referred to a more contemporary form of popular advertising.

The really significant connection between posters and fine art came with the new American painting, and in particular with the size and flatness of these giant murals. Perhaps large paintings and large billboards were together expressive of a new immense continent forming a scale of visual imagery to suit its requirements. The paintings were mostly concerned with huge gestures, but at least one of the artists concerned, Willem de Kooning – born in 1906 in Holland, he moved to the United States in 1926 – has given us an interesting account of the effect of large-scale advertising in his work. De Kooning used pages of newspaper to remove surface areas of paint, and the pressure of the sheets left a faint imprint of the newspaper images – bathing beauties and small ads – on his work. If these passages were later left uncovered then some of the actual mass media material strayed into his painting. The sometimes pathetic details of domestic intimacy revealed by deodorant and lavatory-paper manufacturers produced a concept of banality that intrigued de Kooning. He was fascinated by the dummies in shop-windows and the characters from comic-strips and billboards made by unknown designers and craftsmen without artistic pretensions. There is a long account of de Kooning's interest in this aspect of the consumer society in the introduction by Thomas B. Hess to an exhibition of his work in London in 1968. Hess writes that the series *Woman*, of the 1950s, was conceived in terms of big advertising for a big audience:

> de Kooning was thinking about the American female idols in cigarette advertisements (in one study . . . he cut out the mouth from a 'Be kind to your T-zone' Camel ad and pasted it on the face), the girls whose photographs are paraded through the city on the sides of mail trucks, pinup girls with their extraordinary breasts (a particularly lush example hung in his studio). Thus Woman's ironic presence was modified by his understanding of our modern icons; the Black Goddess has a come-hither smile.

In England, Richard Smith, whose paintings of the late 1950s explored the immense size of beer glasses and cigarette packs, raised the question of whether it was possible to separate the method from the content – and then proceeded to demonstrate that a whole body of work could be made on this assumption:

> I paint about communications. The communications media are a large part of my landscape. My interest is not so much in the message as in the method. There is a multiplicity of messages (smoke these, vote this, ban that), fewer methods. Can how something is communicated be divorced from what is being communicated, and can it be divorced from who it is being communicated to? We tend to look at primitive art in this way, we are unaware of the object's orientation socially and spiritually.

213   When enlarged, the page-size advertisement has a new significance on the street, 1970. (Photo: David Hockney)

On the subject of Pop Art and the popular, a statement by Roy Lichtenstein appeared in an interview with Gene Swenson in 1963. Asked 'What is Pop Art?' he replied:

> I don't know – the use of commercial art as subject matter in painting I suppose. It was hard to get a painting that was despicable enough so that no one could hang it – everybody was hanging everything. It was almost acceptable to hang a dripping paint rag, everybody was accustomed to this. The one thing everybody hated was commercial art; apparently they didn't hate that enough either.

As a statement of a painter's concern with the eternal search for material that does not already have the deadening aura of acceptable taste, this comment by Lichtenstein is straightforward and honest. It does, however, suggest that there is something spurious about the whole operation, which, although this is partly the intention of Lichtenstein's remark, also tends to obscure the perfectly valid sources of his art – the film cartoon and the magazine strip.

203

*214 YOSHITARO ISAKA Poster for TBS Radio, Japan

215 TSUNETOMI KITANO Poster for Takashima department store 1929

216 This artificial world, created by the advertiser from reality, has produced its own mythology which we, as public, are expected to accept as our reality. Artists such as Mel Ramos, Wayne Thiebaud, Tom Wesselmann and Claes Oldenburg have made use of billboard imagery as a basis for their art. In his painting *Smoke Dream No. 2* and his *Highway* series, Allan D'Arcangelo uses the effect of the actual position of billboards in the landscape and the strange combination of the enlarged realistic image and the natural world.

POSTERS AND COMEDY

Humour is used frequently in advertising for the obvious reason that comedy is an essential ingredient of life, and its association with a product extends friendliness and goodwill. Its application is also universal, and light-hearted foolery, like the presence of a court

216 MEL RAMOS *Catsup Queen* 1965

217 SUSUMI EGUCHI Poster for science exhibition for children in a department store 1968

jester, is a valuable outlet in a complicated world. There is also something memorable about a pun or a subtle twist of meaning. 'Take the family for a spin' advises a poster for the prevention of accidents: and the resulting picture is likely to be retained in the mind whereas the tragic documentary evidence of a collision is pushed away by the memory.

Posters, as we have seen, evolved partly from the printed book-plate and partly from circus ephemera; evidence of the comic appears in both these sources. One of the earliest examples from the printed page appears in 1831 in an advertisement for a volume by Dr Ludoff de Garbenfeld against tobacco. It shows a girl suffering through the addiction of her suitor to a pipe, and another victim who is himself a sick man through smoking. Its counterpart is an advertisement of 1866 for *Les Pipes Aristophane*, in which pipes are

205

218   JOSEPH W. MORSE *Five Celebrated Clowns* (woodcut) 1856

given human properties; it includes an orchestra of pipes. Both these examples appear in Ernest Maindron's *Les Affiches Illustrées*, Volume I, of 1886. In the same volume there is a reproduction of an illustrated advertisement of 1702 in which the artist shows an orchestra of cats. This sort of humour, which these early announcements share with the picture postcard, was carried into the first poster designs. Circus and music-hall posters, of course, contained the clowning buffoonery of the actual performance; an example of this humour is used in the poster by Léon Choubrac for the *Cirque Fernando: Bal Masqué*.

In Austria, a popular humorous poster was the type that showed inebriated men at a mass beer-drinking party. There are many variations of this by Schliessmann in works that he made in 1889. The same level of humour is reached by the mass baby-groups that also had such success on picture postcards at the time. A montage of baby bodies with adult heads superimposed appeared as a poster for the *Exhibition of Industrial Art* at Nuremberg in 1896. England, however, seems to have been particularly associated with humour in posters – a fact that Nikolaus Pevsner noted in 1936 in an essay on the subject of the non-serious approach of much Anglo-Saxon design compared with work on the Continent. In England, humour was the great popular leveller and it was applied to most areas of advertising. As we have seen, the entertainment posters of Paris in the 1890s (Chéret and Toulouse-Lautrec) were translated into the English idiom through the work of Dudley Hardy and John Hassall.

219 JEAN D'YLEN
Spa-Monopole 1924

SPA-MONOPOLE
L'EAU QUI PÉTILLE

220   DUDLEY HARDY *A Night Out: 'Oh What a Night!'* c. 1897

Although their posters have suffered by comparison with French designs, one has to appreciate that their real strength lay in the fact that their designs were on the very popular level of comedy, and that far from achieving the homogeneity of the work of an artist like Toulouse-Lautrec, they produced designs that underlined the particular. A patriotic English critic at the time even tried to maintain that the versatility of Hardy was superior to the monotony of Chéret. One of Hassall's most compelling posters was his design for
233   *Skegness* (1909). Hardy's posters vary in style from the assurance of
37   *A Gaiety Girl* (1895) to the particular design of *Oh! What a Night!* –
220   a characteristic poster that represents a certain type of English stage comedy still in existence.

208

221   ROBERT BAILEY *Little Bo-peep Rode a Cycle c.* 1898

222   L. A. MAUZAN *Mago* 1924

Kinderschuhe
Humanic

S 12.— № 26–30
S 15.— № 31–35

KOSEL-GIBSON
WIEN I.

TH J WEINER, WIEN

223   KOSEL-GIBSON *Humanic* 1928

During the 1920s and '30s, the comic strip and the movie cartoon became new influences in visual humour, and these two elements were apparent in poster design. Mauzan's poster for *Mago* (1924), and Kosel-Gibson's design *Humanic* (1928) show evidence of these new effects. In 1927 Savignac produced his cartoon-like design, *Mon Savon*: the extrovert, simple idea of the image has been used ever since by designers wishing to produce a clear-cut expression to show surprise, delight, astonishment, happiness, and so on. Charles

226

211

224   JOHN GILROY *Guinness for Strength* 1934 ▶

225   WILL OWEN *Bisto* ▶

GUINNESS
FOR STRENGTH

*226 RAYMOND SAVIGNAC *Ma Colle* 1950s

Loupot and Cassandre both used comic-strip devices of this sort. A similar approach to humour was followed later by designers in England: the work of Tom Eckersley and Abram Games followed the same pattern. During the Second World War, the cartoon style of a *Punch* artist like Kenneth Bird (Fougasse) was used for posters that warned against 'careless talk'.

In the years following the war this type of design continued to represent the principal means of expressing a comic situation. But there was a sharp change in the nature of humour itself during the 1950s, which has continued to develop. This is the use of 'black' or 'sick' humour. This change of emphasis was not confined to posters

140

but was also noticeable in stage and movie comedies. *Kind Hearts and Coronets* from Britain, *La Traversée de Paris* from France and *Sedotta e Abbandonata* from Italy all reflect a general acceptance of black comedy. Some of the productions of these and other comedies have also produced posters in the same idiom to advertise them. The posters of Heinz Edelmann are characteristic examples of this humour.

With the increased general interest in the bizarre, the images in posters during the 1960s became more far-fetched, and attempts to shock, or to reveal a lack of inhibition on the part of the advertiser

227 HEINZ EDELMANN
Poster for Luis Buñuel film *The Exterminating Angel* 1968

228   PETER BLAKE *Madame Tussaud's* 1968

or designer, left nothing to the imagination. The kind of humour
that had developed in England, for example, in the seaside postcards
of Donald McGill, now became source material for the more
sophisticated satirical reviews and the posters issued by their presses.
The Underground Press, with posters by artists like Martin Sharp,
produced pornographic versions of vernacular humour, most of
which took on exaggerated fantasy. Many of these posters are
deliberately amateurish in appearance – in contrast to the style and
wit, say, of Beardsley's drawings for *Lysistrata*. A great deal of the
humour in the Underground posters is playing on the contrast
between this new alternative society and the Establishment – in
order to show how unrestrained one side can be in contrast to the
monstrous character of traditional social order. Black humour tells

229   OTTOKAR STAFL *Baška c.* 1914 ▶

BAŠKA

230 Posters on display in Margate, Kent. (See also Ill. 205–07, and 231) *c.* 1908

of war and extermination, of love, life and death all at once in pictorial terms that are both fantastic and plausible. Much of the nonsensical humour of the Dadaists that was black indeed seems to have been adapted to an emphatic statement. Absurdity itself is proposed as a positive force, instead of a negative emptiness.

Commercial poster advertising has also been affected by this change of climate: much of its style is camp. Camp has been described as the answer to the problem: how to be a dandy in the age of mass culture. The nineteenth-century dandy affecting refined boredom has been replaced in the twentieth by a camp attitude. This has taken the form of adopting a position that delights in elevating some faded, fantastic or failed element to the level of an art work of consequence. Both the dandy of Huysmans' novels and the camp attitude of today prescribe an aesthetic solution to life's problems. The re-presentation of *Kitsch* consumer art by the painter or the camp re-presentation of highly stylized works of art (like much of Art Nouveau) can both demand a certain love and sympathy for the original on the part of those re-interpreting.

228

218

231 London posters in the 1890s ▶

232   GEORGES MEUNIER *Automobiles Ader* 1913

233   JOHN HASSALL *Skegness Is So Bracing* 1909 ▶

The poster became established in society as a means of display and as an item for collectors. It was the industrialized world of the late nineteenth century that made its appearance a technical possibility, and between 1870 and the end of the First World War posters were associated with art and commerce. With the exception of Chéret's work and the posters of such artists as Toulouse-Lautrec and Mucha, whose designs contributed to art movements in painting, posters in general reflected fashionable styles of decoration or spoke with the language most likely to appeal to all. They were used during this time in politics and war, but because of the prevailing convention of what a poster was expected to be, the directives of those in power were presented within the accepted limits. This situation changed at the end of the First World War; the various political upheavals in Russia and elsewhere determined a new direction for the political poster. This change, however, was not appreciated by many governments – or even by those producing poster designs. The result has been that, even until the 1950s, political posters could still appear to be orientated towards the idea that they are only part of commercial persuasion or an 'artistic' form of advertisement. Perhaps the anachronism is best illustrated in Seymour Chwast's satirical anti-war poster – *War is good business – invest your son*. We are therefore faced with two distinct phases in the history of the ideological poster, the first from 1870 to 1919, when advertising for war was considered in terms of commercial advertising, and the second phase, from 1919 until the present, when the true political poster started to make its appearance.

The war posters of the First World War invariably presented the conflict as a crusade. They fell into two broad categories – those concerned with recruitment, and those that solicited money in terms of the War Loan. In addition there was a category of posters showing war atrocities, in which each side presented a villainous picture of the other. In this respect these posters were certainly outside the usual commerical formula on which posters in general were based.

The most often quoted recruitment poster was that designed in
Great Britain by Alfred Leete, *Your Country Needs You*, with a   *237*
direct, pointing finger and an uncompromising frontal attack that
was one of many similar approaches (for example, the famous one
in the United States by Montgomery Flagg). Leete's poster, however crude it may seem, is succinct; he gives us the head, pointing
finger and hand down to the cuff, but no more. In fact one is
conscious only of the eyes and the tip of the finger of Lord Kitchener,
the Recruiting General: it is sufficient. In fact, although this design
has become a joke, its message has continued as an unmistakable
reminder of that war. Other designs represented the struggle as a
chivalrous affair – both sides calling on the image of St George. The
posters of Käthe Kollwitz and of Faivre, in *On les aura!* (1916), are   *240*
examples of well-drawn, stirring designs that are reminiscent of
Delacroix's *Liberty Guiding the People*. Romantic imagery was also
used in the United States when Fred Spear produced his poster
showing a drowning mother and baby as a result of the sinking of
the *Lusitania*. In Germany, Hohlwein produced a number of war   *236*
posters that show great humanity – his designs were frequently
concerned with prisoners of war, the wounded and the veterans.
Leading designers in Germany – Bernhard, Gipkens and Erdt – also
designed war posters.

Because of the seriousness of war, the lightweight element
associated with household grocery posters was felt to be out of place.
As an alternative to heroics, posters for war were designed in the
other main form expected of them – the art poster. In Great Britain,
Frank Brangwyn and Spencer Pryse produced documentary-style   *244*
lithographed designs that gave a faithful and horrific account of the
miseries of trench life. Pryse even carried lithographic stones with
him in order to make his designs on the spot. By contrast, many of
the war posters were compiled by printers, with very little regard for
the relationship of image to lettering. In the United States a hint
of the form of poster advertising that appeared after the war was
shown in the work of Charles Dana Gibson (creator of the 'Gibson
Girl') and Howard Chandler Christy. American publicity had a
reputation even then, for as early as 1886 Ernest Maindron had

JULIUS USSY ENGELHARD / PLAKAT.

LITHOGRAPHIE UND DRUCK VON DR. C. WOLF & SOHN, MÜNCHEN

234   JULIUS ENGELHARD *Delka* 1918

235   JAN LENICA *Wozzeck* 1964 ▶

236 FRED SPEAR *Enlist* 1915　　　　237 ALFRED LEETE *Your Country Needs You* 1914

referred to it with the words 'nos maîtres en publicité'. Christy used the image of a girl, painted in fresh, painterly brush-strokes, to encourage volunteers: 'Gee! I wish I were a man', says the girl in sailor's uniform, standing to attention in a stiff breeze. '*I want you for*
239 *the Navy*' was another Christy challenge in the popular idiom.

The most significant development in the history of political posters and one of the most important in the whole history of the medium, occurred at that time in Russia. In 1919 a new type of poster appeared there which is said to have been the work originally of Mikhail Cheremnykh. It was known as the 'Satire window of the Russian Telegraph Agency' (the title of this organization is usually abbreviated to the initials ROSTA). The windows consisted of illustrations with captions that resemble the cinematic sequence of the comic strip. The most famous of these designs are those made by
242 the poet Mayakovsky: some of them include up to fourteen narrative illustrations with captions like sub-titles, usually stencilled. Camilla Gray-Prokofieva has noted the influence of the sacred icon and the

A HÁBORU BORZALMAI ELLEN
BUDAPEST MUNKÁSSÁGA VASÁRNAP D.U.
TÜNTETŐ FELVONULÁST ÉS NÉPGYÜLÉST
TART A TATTERSAALBAN.

MINDEN MUNKÁSNAK TILTAKOZNI
KELL A TÖMEGMÉSZÁRLÁS ELLEN
A MAGYARORSZÁGI SZOCIÁLDEMOKRATA PÁRT.

38   MICHAEL BIRO SDP anti-war poster 1914

O JULES-ABEL FAIVRE *On les aura!* 1916

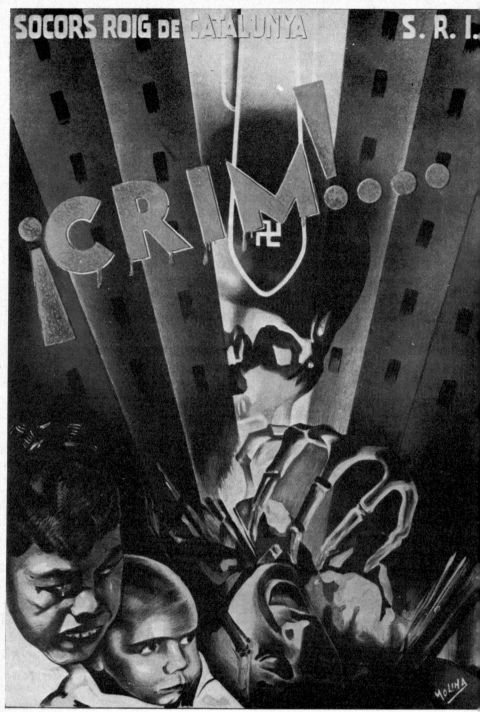

241   MOLINA Spanish Civil War poster 1937

lubok (a Russian folk-art design, popular until the end of the nineteenth century), with its combination of text and illustration, on the work of Larionov and Goncharova. From this connection Mayakovsky, who had become associated with the renewed interest in native folk-art traditions, himself developed this remarkable combination of poetry and image. It is significant that the production of these designs was later carried out as a joint co-operative effort and that copies could be made and distributed rapidly for display in the 'windows', each bulletin being numbered, and therefore creating a sequence and pattern of information. The collective method of making posters is also paralleled in Berlin by the November Group, founded in 1918 by Max Pechstein and Hans Richter.

Constructivism has already been discussed as a formal art movement which influenced poster design, but its political significance has not been mentioned. Clearly there were two revolutions – an artistic one and a political one. That there were strong links is shown, for example, by the fact, that mass distribution of bulletins and propaganda (as in the Agit-Prop trains that printed and distributed information) was carried out by and for the Revolution. The 'window' technique of the ROSTA posters was also later built into the *avant-garde* architecture of newspaper buildings by A. Vesnin, that include provision for large screens on which front-page news would be projected daily. In the West it is widely thought that the new, startling designs of *avant-garde* art were synonymous with the new Soviet world. From the very start, however, Lenin hated the Russian Futurists and found the bohemian life and strange experiments of Mayakovsky an embarrassment to the idealistic aims of the Revolution. The *avant-garde* artists themselves either chose to remain in Russia where their work became less vital, went into exile, or committed suicide; a few were sent to labour camps. The whole movement ceased to have any consequence in the country of its origin, although its effects contributed to the development of art in other countries. The combined work of painter and poet was one of the products of the Revolution that made a real contribution to the history of posters, and promises to develop further in the future with the increasing interdependence of the arts.

231

1) В ШИКАРНОМ ВАГОНЕ
В ВАГОНЕ САЛОНЕ
ТРИ ФРАНЦУЗА ЕДУТ И
ВЕДУТ МЕЖ СОБОЙ БЕСЕДУ.

2) ГОВОРИТ НУЛАНС ТРЯСЯСЬ ОТ
СМЕХА "ВОТ БУДЕТ ПОТЕХА -

3) КАК ДОЕДЕМ ДО ГОЛОДНЫХ
МЕСТ СРАЗУ ВЫПУСТИМ МАНИФЕСТ

4) КТО ХОЧЕТ ЕСТЬ ВСЛАСТЬ
СВЕРГАЙ СОВЕТСКУЮ ВЛАСТЬ.

5) ВОТ ВАМ ЦАРЬ ВОТ ЦАРИЦА
А ВОТ РОЖЬ И ПШЕНИЦА.

6) ГОВОРИТ ЖИРО
ПОДМИГНУВ ХИТРО

7) ЭТОГО МАЛО —
МЫ ИХ ПОТРЯСЕМ СНАЧАЛА

8) ПУСТЬ ПОПОТЕЮТ КАК СЛЕДУЕТ
А ПОТОМ ПООБЕДАЮТ

9) ГОВОРИТ ПО-ГЕНЕРАЛ БРАВЫЙ
ЗНАЕМ КОРМИШЬ ВСЕЙ ОРАВОЙ.

10) МЫ ИХ ЧИСЛОМ ПОУБАВИМ
ТИХИХ ОСТАВИМ.

11) А КТО С НОРОВОМ ВЗДОРНЫМ
— ТОГО ВЗДЕРНЕМ.

12) ДРУЗЬЯ РАСХОДИТЕСЬ ОЧЕННО
РОССИЯ-НЕ ВАША ВОТЧИНА.

Свободн.Нар.Просвет. 316.

LA ODISEA DEL GRAL JOSE

DIRECCION: JORGE FRAGA
CON: ...
JOSE ANTONIO RODRIGUEZ
...
FILM CUBANO

Nico 69

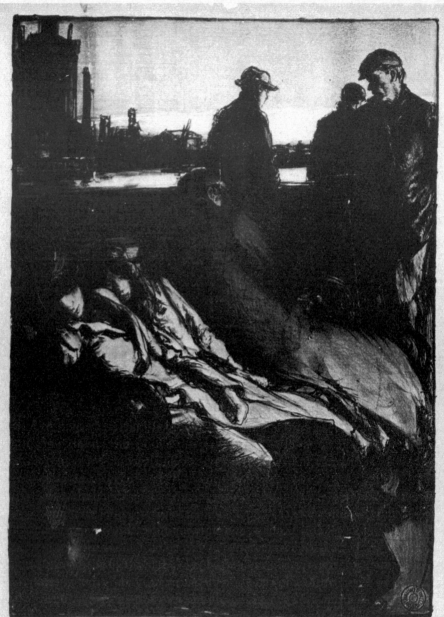

244 GERALD SPENCER PRYSE *Workless* 1910

ANONYMOUS British Labour Party poster 1934

par tous les temps

*248   XANTI *Mussolini* 1934

249   MANCHE Nazi recruiting poster used in Netherlands

The work of collective organizations in producing posters appeared again in Republican and Communist posters in Madrid and Barcelona in 1936 during the Civil War in Spain. Posters during the Civil War demonstrated new techniques, such as photomontage. The Fascist regimes that supported Franco's forces during that war had been making use of propaganda systems in the years just preceding it. Some of the official designs for Mussolini's regime consisted of monolithic three-dimensional sets, composed of lettering, that echoed the architectural splendours of Imperial Rome. Some of these constructions were used in commercial advertising: the architectural construction by Fortunato Depero for Campari in 1933 and designs in the Salone del Motore of 1931 by Piero Todeschini. The work by Seneca for Buitoni Pasta also has the same character, and posters for Fiat cars use the familiar technique publicized all over the world in the design for the introduction of Twentieth Century-Fox films from Hollywood. The poster by Xanti for Mussolini

248

238

250   VOSKUIL Poster for exhibition commemorating the Olympic Games under Nazi patronage 1936 ▶

de olympiade onder dictatuur
entoonstelling:
sport, kunst, wetenschap, documenten

amsterdam
augustus
1936
gebouw
de geelvinck
singel 530

appears by comparison as conventional rhetoric. In Germany 'National Socialist Realism' was echoed in posters such as Voskuil's 250 *Olympics* 1936. However, all the war posters of the thirties are reduced to insignificance beside the mural painted by Picasso for the Spanish Pavilion at the Paris Exposition of 1937. *Guernica* can hardly be called a poster but when we recall the influence that poster design, with its emphasis on simple dramatic forms, may have had on Picasso's early work, we can see that this great mural outstripped any of the gargantuan billboards or advertising displays, and that Picasso had with great daring made use of his discoveries of the previous thirty years in this painting that measures over 25 × 11 feet.

HENRI MONTASSIER *La Machine à Finir la Guerre* 1917–18

253 MIECZSLAW TOMKIEWICZ *To the West!*
1945

254 ANONYMOUS *Assassin* (anti-American po
issued in France by the Nazis) 1943

The posters produced during the Second World War did not add anything to the achievements already established in the development of poster design generally. Mass communication methods had changed and propaganda flowed through the cinema and the radio. Consumer advertising was cut and posters showed the civilians of total war how to grow food, conserve their supplies and guard the secrets of their respective countries. Some distinguished work appeared in the United States from Ben Shahn, Henry Koerner, Glen Grohe and Jean Carlu. In Russia, Mikhail Kuprianov, Porfiry Krylov and Nikolai Sokolov produced a number of posters that were in the tradition of Russian cartoon and folk art.

Since 1945 a significant change in world opinion about war has
259 caused a great deal of publicity to be given to anti-war posters.

KÄTHE KOLLWITZ *No More War* 1924

255 Käthe Kollwitz's poster *No More War* (1924) has found a tragic echo
246 in *No More Hiroshimas!* (1968) by Hirokatsu. But this change is one of
content rather than style, for the use of realism or satire as a means
of deterrent in advertising has not added anything to the appearance
of posters. A new form is achieved when a special type of design
appears, perhaps, for example, because the posters are prepared by a
minority group within a hostile majority, in which case the printing,
distribution and posting has to be a clandestine operation – a fact
that will affect their design and style.

The Paris rising in May 1968 was such an occasion, and after a
hundred years of respectable development the poster suddenly
appeared as a young, virile medium in the city where it had first been
developed. Once again, as in the production of the ROSTA posters
of the Russian Revolution, a cooperative system of choosing designs
and printing them was shared by professionals as well as the in-
experienced. The resulting series of posters was designed for use –
any attempt to turn the output into a collectors' market was resisted
by the students of the Beaux-Arts who were responsible for the
work. The posters have the character of hastily prepared broadsheets: they brought back a feeling of urgency to a medium that, for
instant information, had been superseded by radio and television. If
coverage is not available on the complicated technical system of
mass communications, then posters can have a strong effect –
especially if they return to their primitive state instead of being the
tasteful art works to which the public have become accustomed.

In the introduction to a collection of these works in book form,
Usine-Université-Union states that 'experience has taught us the
danger of ambiguity and the necessity of incorporating slogans as an
integral part of that design. Sincerity, fantasy, are only effective when
they interpret and reinforce the attack made by the slogan.'

In describing the Atelier Populaire the article says:

[It] consists of a workshop where the posters are conceived, and
several workshops where they are produced (printing by the silk-
screen process, lithography, stencilling, dark-room and so on).
All the militants – workers, students, artists, etc. from the Atelier

Populaire meet daily in a general Assembly. The work of this Assembly is not merely to choose between the designs and slogans suggested for posters, but also to discuss all political problems.

The main difficulty was to avoid endless discussion and to allow the process of designing and printing to move forward; the communal decisions could be added at any point. An example is shown on this page: *La Chienlit c'est lui!* of 19 May 1968 was produced in answer to de Gaulle's 'La Reforme oui, la Chienlit non!' 256

The posters of the Atelier Populaire had the direct impact of word and image; and the whole series maintains the traditions of good poster design – the popular sign and the broadsheet from which the medium grew.

By the end of the 1960s it became apparent that the development of poster design through the channels of commercialism had now

257 Chinese Communist government poster

found a strong alternative area of expression – in the posters of ideologies, whether these represented political ideologies or the ideals of a new generation. The posters, banners and paintings of the Communist government of Red China have made a spectacular contribution to the world history of poster design. As in the West, some of these designs have been developed from popular folk art. In China the *nien hua*, or New Year pictures of the Spring Festival, are part of the traditional Chinese imagery. They have been adapted for Communist ends, as is often the case with designs in the popular idiom: Communist iconography has been added to the folk image. At the moment, one wonders how successful this assimilation of propaganda is in such a popular form of expression. For example, the appeal of traditional designs is probably of greater significance than the added details of Party symbolism; in time, some of these elements will themselves become part of the tradition. The most exciting designs from China are the giant images of Party leaders and Party symbols. 257 In their way, they are of course comparable to the large-scale commercial advertising in the United States, but the propaganda of the East is different from that of the West – its imagery has not produced the same degree of banality. Perhaps this is because its methods are slower and less sophisticated, and the results must appeal to a society that is still concerned with more traditional, basic requirements. Political Pop Art in countries like Tibet, as well as in the Latin American states, still belongs to the traditional means of display. The United States, by contrast, has produced a society which created its own folk myths from the mass media – these images have been projected all over the world into cultures of varying degrees of development.

Nowhere has this dual influence been felt more acutely than in Cuba – so close to the United States geographically but so distant in terms of culture and ideology. The posters of the Cuban Revolution have become justly famous, and the most interesting aspect of this sudden flowering of talent lies precisely in the duality of posters that borrow their style from the West and their message from the East. Cuban designers have been given much more freedom of expression than one has come to associate with a society based on Communism. Their posters include frequent quotations from the commercial advertisement and from psychedelic, Pop Art, comic-strip and film posters of the United States consumer society. There are also quotations from Picasso and from the theatrical posters of Poland. A number of works exist that deliberately confuse images produced in different situations but which have a visual link in other ways. The colour red for example is the link in an image showing a face smeared with blood but which suggests that it is a lipstick advertisement.

The contrast of tough brutality, on the one hand, and the fashion still on the other, is echoed in the paintings of Erro (the Icelandic artist Gundmunder Gundmundsson) – in a series from the late 1960s. In this the contrast is made between the suburban interior, with its 'Sears Roebuck' furnishings and its apparent invasion by Viet-Cong guerrillas. This is achieved by representing one wall of

End Bad Breath.

the trim, domestic scene as a poster-mural which literally spills out into the room. The same idea of using two elements is given the more familiar combination of sex with violence in William Weege's *Fuck the CIA!* (1967), a poster from the United States.

Poster work in Cuba has been described by Edmundo Desnoes, the Cuban writer and critic:

> In the houses, on the walls and windows, the new posters and billboards have replaced the painting of a flamingo, the North American calendar, magazines and advertisements for consumer goods and have introduced a new vision, a new pre-occupation, without appealing to or exploiting sensationalism, sex or the illusion of aristocratic life.

'The illusion of aristocratic life' has done a great deal to make the poster generally seem to be linked forever to consumer society advertising. The development of an alternative body of poster designs in Cuba to that of the consumer society, that nevertheless makes use of contemporary design ideas, has given posters a new justification.

In examining the contribution of these posters we must realize that their editions are limited by the technical problems of reproduction. Thus their rarity has given them a high market value – although those responsible for producing them have maintained that no collector's market exists, that the posters are used and enjoyed and then perish. It is also interesting that frequently they are not designed out of a need to 'sell' anything. Even cinema posters, which form an important section of this output, are virtually unnecessary for, although there are many cinemas in Havana, they are attended to capacity in any case. The ideological posters are displays by a socialist society for a socialist society, and the competitive hysteria of Western commercial advertising is absent from them. In addition, all poster artists in Cuba are employed by the government in various agencies.

Cuban poster designers are freer of official restrictions than those in Soviet Russia or Red China. In both latter countries, strict limitations are placed on the nature of the designs and, in the case of China, there are precise conventions that define the actual method of interpretation. The posters also reflect the total anonymity of communal decisions about their composition. In Cuba all traditions in the history of poster design are open to the individual designer, and a survey of recent poster design in that country reveals that artists have made full use of the established language of the poster from one end of the

LONG LIVE THE THIRD COMMUNIST INTERNATIONAL! VIVE LA TROISIÈME INTERNATIONALE COMMUNISTE! EVVIVA IL TERZA INTERNAZIONALE COMUNISTA! ES LEBE DIE DRITTE KOMMUNISTISCHE INTERNATIONALE!

*260   ANONYMOUS *Long Live the Third Communist International*

world to the other and from the whole hundred years' range of the   *243*
poster's existence.

Such plagiarism might sound as though Cuba had produced a
weary anthology of trends – like some international design award
annual – but the Cuban posters are unique because of the fusion of
the decorative styles of the West without the incessant economic
pressure. The result is often a design in which the creative expression
of the painter approaches the language of communication associated
elsewhere with the work of professional graphic designers. This development has reached impressive heights in the large, simple designs
expressing the spirit of the Revolution. The bringing together of fine

OTHER HANDS WILL TAKE UP THE WEAPONS

261 ANONYMOUS
Cuban political poster
with English title 1970

arts and graphic arts is described by Adelaide de Juan in *Cuba Internacional* in July 1969:

> By narrowing the division between both groups of people [those who go to museums and those who do not] we narrow equally the division in the idea that claims the existence of two plastic manifestations, one for the learned and one for the ignorant. . . . An easel painting is intimate as much for the spectator as for the painter. . . . There is, furthermore, the idea that the painting is the painter's (his ideas, his problems, his joy) while graphic work (billboards, book covers, magazines, posters) is informational and is consequently indebted to the movies, the theatre, to ideas, etc., and remains subjected to a theme which did not originate with the artist; it is work executed on demand. To all this we must add the

act of the personal touch in the execution of the painting, and the collective work in the production of graphics. . . . There is no distinction in quality between the utilitarian and the artistic work. The more artistic a graphic work is, the more useful it is. Of course all art work better fits its purpose when it transcends its original function. . . . The established stylistic interrelation between graphics and painting is part of a growing tendency which will be useful in making their differences disappear.

(Translation by Dugald Stermer in *The Art of Revolution*, 1970)

One of Cuba's prominent painters, Raúl Martinez, has turned his attention increasingly towards graphic work. From his paintings he has developed designs that seem to have a connection with indigenous *262* Cuban art forms. As in the development of posters in most countries from France to China, a connection has had to be made in the folk art of the country in order to find a real means of popular expression.

262 RAÚL MARTINÉZ Painting 1966

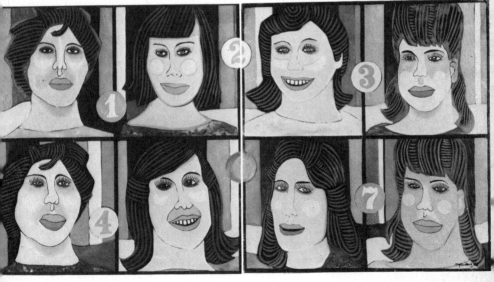

(The Pop Art of consumer advertising constitutes a camp style that is entertaining but of too recent origin.) Martinez' poster *Lucía* shows how this traditional Cuban style acts as a basis for more recent influences; the result is less of a pastiche than some of the other quotations made in Cuban posters from different sources. Martinez has turned away from painting towards graphic design because he feels more in touch with the people in this way. He has been quoted as saying: 'Up to now, painting in general aims towards responses and solutions of problems which the artist himself has posed, whereas the graphic artist answers the problems that are put to him.' In fact, in all parts of the world today, objects and attitudes in painting and sculpture are moving towards mass-communication methods. Conversely, advertising, as always, makes excursions into styles that are developed in the fine arts. Chairman Mao has said: 'we are against . . . the tendency to produce works in the "slogan and poster" style which are correct in their political views but are weak in artistic expression. We must, in literature and art, conduct the struggle on two fronts.'

The two fronts are moving closer together; perhaps in Cuba there is only one front. For many years, Soviet Russia pursued the policy of producing heroic posters and paintings in the naturalist style, and it is against this tendency that the Cuban situation has been evolved. In 1925 Lenin, whose views on certain attitudes of the *avant-garde* have already been mentioned, said: 'Art belongs to the people. Its roots should penetrate deeply into the very thick masses of the people. It should be comprehensible to these masses and loved by them.' What the Russian masses, however, were getting in poster design, as well as in painting, was a form of strict naturalism. John Berger has referred to 'Socialist Naturalism masquerading as Socialist Realism' – naturalism in this context being a rather unselective replica, as opposed to realism, which Berger defines as a much more ambitious attempt to grasp total reality. Soviet art was also academic and self-conscious. The masses were being given 'mass-art' from above; they were not allowed to participate; this was not the art of the people. The co-operatives of the old ROSTA window posters, the students' posters of May '68 in Paris – these were attempts to produce a genuine pattern of popular art, even if there was direction.

254

263 ANONYMOUS *WR – The Mysteries of the Organism* (poster for Yugoslav film) 1971 ▶

GASMOTHERAPY. Milena Dravic. Jagoda Kaloper. Ivica Vidovic. Tuli Kupferberg. Zoran Radmilovic. Jackie Curtis. Miodrag Andric. SEXPOL AGITROP. Author. Director. Dusan MAKAVEJEV. WR. ...era. Pega Popovic. Aleksandar Petkovic. NEOPLANTA FILM. Novi Sad. TELEPOOL. München. Collaborators. Bojana. Probst. Ivanka. Sarlo. Special guest. GHOST OF J. V. STALIN. WR. ...elm Reich. WR. World revolution. WR. Joy of LIVING. WR. SOCIALISM with human BODY. What are you doing with your capacity for 4000 ORGASMS in your LIFETIME? WR. Start your DE-REPRESSION with this FILM. FREEDOM and LOVE are inexhaustible. Be ANGRY but don't stop BREATHING! HE WHO CHOOSES HIS SLAVERY IS HE A SLAVE STILL? ...m. 80 minutes. COLOUR!

WR

MISTERIJE ORGANIZMA
LES MYSTÈRES DE L'ORGANISME
DIE MYSTERIEN DES ORGANISMUS
THE MYSTERIES OF ORGANISM

It is important to see that official direction on a large scale produces poster work and painting naturalism that pretend to be reality. In other words, the mirror held up to the public is in fact an image and not a reflection: 'This is how we want you to see yourselves.' The West regards official propaganda in the Soviet Union in this light, the East looks at the consumer society advertising of the capitalist West in an identical way. The popular idiom in advertising ranges from the genuine folk-art image to the 'camp' of mass culture, from the controlled society of the East to the free-for-all of the West.

Art of the people and art for the people may be two different areas of expression. The poster is the means of conveying both graphic messages; whatever its claims as art it must first speak to the people.

264 EMORY DOUGLAS *Trick or Treat* (Black Panther poster) 1970

Three-dimensional posters

The 1970s have seen a renewed emphasis on the inter-relation in the arts between flat design and three-dimensional expression; but it is interesting to realize that poster designs have often been extended from the traditional placard to more plastic forms. The few examples illustrated on the following pages are merely an indication of such work.

In France, at the turn of the century, Mme Yeldo had produced effigies of several famous personalities who had also been featured in poster designs – *Aristide Bruant* is an example. Throughout the period covered by this book, the styles followed in posters have in fact been translated into three dimensions.

In 1924 Herbert Bayer designed a number of kiosks – illustration 267 shows one of them – and suggested that articles should be sold as well as advertised from these miniature exhibition stands. In Italy in 1927 Fortunato Depero made his *Pavilion* (ill. 266), which was commissioned by the firms of Bestetti-Tumminelli and Travers Bros. It appeared at the Third International Exhibition of Decorative Art at Monza in that year, and has been described as 'architectonic typoplasticism'.

Another work is *Miss Blanche* by V. Hussar (ill. 265), which made its appearance in 1927 and which expressed the ideas of De Stijl. Illustrated in the main text is a work of 1935 – Jean Carlu's *Cuisine Électrique* (ill. 96). It consisted of polished aluminium, copper, mosaics in four colours, and neon tubes. Carlu made other examples for different firms.

The *Freak Cars* (ills. 268 and 269) are typical examples of a once common form of advertising and, together with Artur Gumitsch's display objects of the thirties (ills. 270–73), belong to the world of the surrealists.

265 V. HUSSAR *Miss Blanche* (De Stijl display) 1927

266
FORTUNATO DEPER(
Pavilion 1927

267   HERBERT BAYER
Newspaper kiosk
(Bauhaus display) 1924

268 ANONYMOUS Royal Ediswan Lamps. Freak car 1927

269 ANONYMOUS Electrolux Ltd. Freak car 1927

O-73 ARTUR GUMITSCH Milk; hairstylist; shoes; toothpaste. Three-dimensional
splays from the nineteen thirties

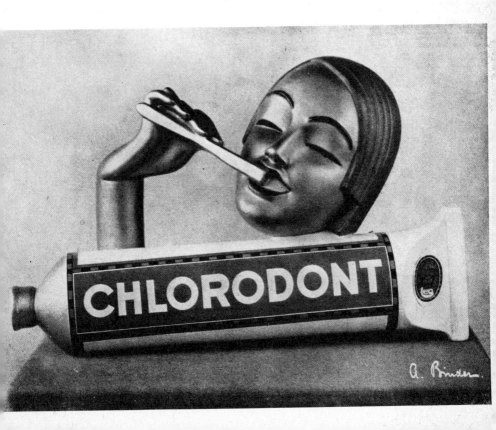

Bibliography

The bibliography lists the books, magazines and exhibition catalogues that have been used in preparing this volume. It is hoped that the list will also act as a source of reference for further reading.

It would be impossible to acknowledge each work in the context in which it has been used but, apart from quotations noted in the text, the information in Chapter Three on the exchanges between Roland Holst and Albert Hahn was taken from *A History of the Dutch Poster, 1890–1960* by Dick Dooijes and Pieter Brattinga (1968).

BOOKS AND SPECIAL ARTICLES

Abdy, Jane *The French Poster* London, 1969

Alquié, Ferdinand *Philosophie du surréalisme* Paris, 1955

Amaya, Mario *Art Nouveau* London, 1966

Amiel, Denys *Les spectacles à travers les ages* (vol. II) Paris, 1931

Amstutz, Walter (ed.) *Who's Who in Graphic Art* Zürich, 1962

Atelier Populaire *Mai '68* London, 1969

Battersby, Martin *The Decorative Twenties* London, 1969

Bauwens, Maurice (ed.) *Les affiches étrangères illustrées* Paris, 1897

Berger, John *Art and Revolution* London, 1969

Browse, Lillian *William Nicholson* London, 1956

Butnik-Siver'sky *Sovietskii Plakat Epokhi 1918–21* Moscow, 1960

Cassou, Jean; Langui, Emil; Pevsner, Nikolaus *Sources of Modern Art* London, 1962

Celant, Germano *Nizzoli* Milan, 1968

Cendrars, Blaise *Le spectacle est dans la rue* Montrouge, 1935

Compton, Michael *Pop Art* Feltham, 1970

Constantine, Mildred *Sign Language for Buildings and Landscape* New York, 1961

Le Corbusier *L'art décoratif d'aujourd'hui* Paris, 1959

Cossío, José María de *Los Toros* (vol. 2) Madrid, 1960

Documentos Historicos Madrid, 1937.

Dooijes, Dick; Brattinga, Pieter *A History of the Dutch Poster, 1890–1960* Amsterdam, 1968

Dorfles, Gillo *Kitsch* London, 1969

Eisner, Lotte *The Haunted Screen* London, 1969

Fujikake, Shizuya *Ukiyoye* Tokyo, 1915

Gasser, Manual *Exempla Graphica* Zürich, 1968

'The Poster Craze' *Graphis* 135, 1968

Gerstner, Karl; Kutter, Markus *The New Graphic Art* London, 1959

Gluck, Felix (ed.) *World Graphic Design* London, 1968

Golding, John *Cubism: A History and an Analysis, 1907–1914* London, 1959

Goldwater, Robert J. 'L'affiche moderne' *Gazette des Beaux-Arts XXIII* Paris, 1942

Gombrich, Ernst H. *Caricature* Harmondsworth, 1940

Psychoanalysis and the History of Art London, 1954

Art and Illusion London, 1960

Meditations on a Hobby Horse London, 1963

Hauser, Arnold *Social History of Art* London, 1951

Haworth-Booth, Mark E. *McKnight Kauffer* (in preparation)

Henrion, Frederick H. K.; Parkin, Alan *Design Co-ordination and Corporate Image* London 1967

Herbert, Robert L. 'Seurat and Jules Chéret' *Art Bulletin* June 1958

Hiatt, Charles *Picture Posters* London, 1895

Hillier, Bevis *Posters* London, 1968

Hofstaetter, Hans H. *Jugendstil Druckkunst* Baden-Baden, 1968

Hudson, Derek *James Pryde* London, 1949

Hutchison, Harold F. *London Transport Posters* London, 1963

The Poster London, 1968

Jaffé, H. L. C. *De Stijl* London, 1970

Kahn, Gustave *L'esthétique de la rue* Paris, 1901

Keen, Graham; La Rue, Michel *Underground Graphics* London, 1970

Koch, Robert 'A Poster by Khnopff', *Marsyas* (vol. 6) 1950–53

Kowalski, Tadeusz *The Polish Film Poster* Warsaw, 1957

Kunzle, David *L'era di Johnson* Milan, 1968

Laver, James *Great Posters of the Past* London, 1942

French XIX-Century Posters London, 1944

Art for All London, 1949

Lepape, Georges *Les Choses de Paul Poiret* Paris, 1911

Lissitzky-Küppers, Sophie *El Lissitzky* London, 1968

Lo Duca, Giuseppe *L'affiche* Paris, 1969

McKnight Kauffer, E. *The Art of the Poster* London, 1924

Maindron, Ernest *Les affiches illustrées* (vol. I, 1886; vol. II, 1896), Paris

Malevich, Kazimir *Essays on Art, 1915–*

28 (edited by T. Andersen) Copenhagen, 1968

Marx, Roger *Les maîtres de l'affiche* (5 vols) Paris, 1896–1900

Mascha, Ottokar *Österreichische Plakatkunst* Vienna, 1915

Mauclair, Camille *Jules Chéret* Paris, 1930

Metzl, Ervine *The Poster: its History and its Art* New York, 1963

Moholy-Nagy, László *The New Vision, from Material to Architecture* (translated by D. M. Hoffmann) London, 1939

Painting, photography, film (translated by J. Seligman) London, 1969

Mondrian, Piet *Plastic Art and Pure Plastic Art, and Other Essays, 1941–43* New York, 1945

Mucha, Jiří *Alphonse Mucha: His Life and Art* London, 1966

Müller-Brockmann, Josef *A History of Visual Communication* Teufen am Rhein, 1971

Neumann, Eckhard *Functional Graphic Design in the 20s* New York, 1967

Olivetti, Camillo *Olivetti 1908–1958* Ivrea, 1958

Ozenfant, Amédée; Jeanneret, C. E. (Le Corbusier) *Après le Cubisme* Paris, 1918

Ozenfant, Amédée *Journey through Life* London, 1939

Foundations of Modern Art New York, 1952

Partito Nazionale Fascista *Mostra della Rivoluzione Fascista* Rome, 1933

Peters, Louis F. *Kunst und Revolte* Cologne, 1968

Pevsner, Nikolaus *Pioneers of the Modern Movement* London, 1936

'The Psychology of English and German Posters' *Penrose Annual XXXVIII*, 1936

Pincus-Witten, Robert 'Ideal Interlude' (Rose + Croix) *Art Forum*, September 1968

Polak, Bettina *Het fin-de-siècle in de*

Nederlandse Schilderkunst The Hague, 1955

Symbolism Amsterdam, 1967

Posada, José Guadalupe *El Fondo Editorial de la Plástica Mexicana* 1963

Rademacher, Hellmut *Deutsche Plakat* Dresden, 1965

Reade, Brian *Art Nouveau and Alphonse Mucha* London, 1963

Beardsley London, 1967

Rheims, Maurice *The Age of Art Nouveau* London, 1966

Rickards, Maurice *Posters at the Turn of the Century* London, 1968

Posters of the First World War London, 1968

Posters of the Nineteen Twenties London, 1968

Banned Posters London, 1969

Posters of Protest and Revolution Bath, 1970

Rookmaaker, Hendrik R. *Synthetist Art Theories* Amsterdam, 1959

Rosenberg, Bernard; White, David M. (eds.) *Mass Culture* London, 1964

Ruben, Paul *Die Reklame* Berlin, 1914

Rublowsky, John *Pop Art* Camden, N.J., 1965

Sailer, Anton *Das Plakat* Munich, 1956

Schardt, Hermann *Paris 1900* London, 1970

Schmutzler, Robert *Art Nouveau* London, 1964

Schubert, Walter F. *Die Deutsche Werbe Graphik* Berlin, 1927

Selz, Peter 'The Hippy Poster' *Graphis* 135, 1968

Sontag, Susan *Against Interpretation and Other Essays* London, 1967

Sovietskii Khudozhnik *Soviet Poster Artists* Moscow, 1949

Spencer, Herbert *Pioneers of Modern Typography* London, 1969

Stermer, Dugald *The Art of Revolution* (with introduction by Susan Sontag) London, 1970

Swiss Poster Art, 1941–65 (von Grunigen and others) Zürich, 1969

Tschichold, Jan *Asymmetric Typography* (translated by Ruari McLean from *Typographische Gestaltung*, 1935) London, 1967

Vox, Maximilien *Cassandre* Ste Gallen, 1948

Waelder, Robert *Psychoanalytic Avenues to Art* London, 1965

Wagner, Geoffrey *Parade of Pleasure* London, 1954

Walker, Cummings C. (ed.) *The Great Poster Trip: Art Eureka* Palo Alto, 1968

Wember, Paul *Die Jugend der Plakate 1887–1917* Krefeld, 1961

Wingler, Hans Maria *The Bauhaus 1919–1933* Cambridge, Mass., 1969

Zur Westen, Walter von *Reklamekunst aus zwei Jahrtausenden* Berlin, 1925

PERIODICALS

Annual of Advertising and Editorial Art and Design New York, 1921

Annuario della Publicità Italiana Bolzano, 1929

Art International d'aujourd'hui Paris, 1928–29

Arts et Métiers Graphiques Paris, 1927–39

CA Magazine Palo Alto, 1959–

Campo Grafico Milan, 1936–39

L'esprit nouveau Paris, 1920–25

Gebrauchsgrafik Berlin, 1924–38; Munich, 1950–

Graphis and *Graphis Annuals* Zürich, 1944–

International Poster Annual Zürich, 1948

Living Arts (ICA London) 1963–64

Neue Graphik Zürich, 1958–65

Das Plakat Berlin, 1912–21

The Poster (later *The Poster and Art Collector*) London, 1898–1901

Posters and their Designers (later *Posters and Publicity*) London, 1924–29

Projekt Warsaw, 1956–

Publicità in Italia Milan, 1957–

Publicité Geneva, 1944–
De Stijl Amsterdam, 1917–32
Ver Sacrum Vienna, 1898; Leipzig, 1899–
1903

SELECT LIST OF EXHIBITION CATALOGUES
Barcelona, Palacio de la Virretna:
'Exposicion Ramon Casas' 1958
Berkeley, California, University Art
Gallery: 'Jugendstijl and Expression-
ism in German Posters' 1965
Brussels, Musées Royaux des Beaux-
Arts: 'Le groupe de XX et son temps'
1962
Edinburgh, The Waverley Market:
'Olivetti Concept and Form' 1970
New York, Museum of Modern Art:
'Cubism and Abstract Art' 1936

'Bauhaus' 1938
'Art Nouveau' 1959
'Word and Image' 1968
Paris, Bibliothèque Nationale: 'Cinq
siècles d'affiches françaises' 1953
Paris, Musée des Arts Décoratifs: 'A. M.
Cassandre de 1925 à 1950' 1950
'Push Pin' 1970
Stockholm, Nationalmuseet: 'Svenska
Affischtecknare' 1954
Toronto, Art Gallery of Ontario: 'Sacred
and Profane in Symbolist Art' 1969
Vienna, Bundösterreichischer Geb-
rauchsgraphiker: 'Österreichische
Plakate 1890–1957' 1957
Warsaw, Central Bureau of Art Exhibi-
tions: 'Polish Biennale I', 1966
'Polish Biennale II' 1968
'Polish Biennale III' 1970

List of Illustrations

Special acknowledgment is made to: Peter Adam, for allowing a painting by Martinez and recent Cuban posters to be photographed; David Hockney, for lending photographs of billboards; the staffs of the Stedelijk Museum, Amsterdam, and the Library and Print Room of the Victoria and Albert Museum, London, for their help in tracing and providing material.

Fragonard and Correggio. In addition, there were reproductions of the work of Degas, Rodin and Besnard – a winner of the Prix de Rome and described by Cézanne as 'that pompier who's always on fire'. Chéret's studio also contained busts by Houdon and casts after Michelangelo and Donatello. Chéret also made casts from the limbs of dancers and, after 1889, casts from Javanese dancers who took part in the Exposition of that year and for whom he made a poster. A comparison of illustrations 2 and 6 shows a striking connection between Chéret's art and that of one of his sources.
Sketch for a painting in the Cathedral at Este. Oil on canvas
Metropolitan Museum of Art, Pogos Fund, 1937

7 HENRI DE TOULOUSE-LAUTREC
Reine de Joie 1892
Reine de Joie, Mœurs du demi-monde was a novel by Victor Jozé (Victor Dosky, a Polish writer). It formed part of a series, *La Ménagerie Sociale*.
Victoria and Albert Museum, London

8 THOMAS THEODOR HEINE
Simplicissimus 1897
V.E.B. Verlag der Kunst, Dresden

9 Bartholomew Fair, London 1721
Guildhall Art Gallery, London

10 WILHELM LISZT
Ver Sacrum Kalender 1903

11 LUDWIG VON ZUMBUSCH
Cover for Jugend (No. 40) 1897

12 JULES CHÉRET
Les Girard 1879
Collection of the Museum of Modern Art, New York. Acquired by exchange

13 ALPHONSE MUCHA
Papier Job 1897

14 ALPHONSE MUCHA
Gismonda 1894
Mucha was asked to design this poster for Sarah Bernhardt at very short notice, there being no one else available at the printer Lemercier when her order was suddenly received. Bernhardt was delighted with the originality of the design, and Mucha subsequently did many works for her. The lower half of the poster was left incomplete as there was not sufficient time to continue the detailed patterns, which are based on Byzantine designs.

15 VICTOR SCHUFINSKY
Lucifer Girl 1904
Stedelijk Museum, Amsterdam

16 ANONYMOUS
Circus programme *c.* 1864
While in England, Chéret became friendly with a group of clowns and obviously knew a great deal about circus life. An anonymous poster for such a group exists – *The Phoites*; its composition closely resembles that of Chéret's *Les Girard* (ill. 12). The triple design shown here for Le Cirque Rancy is typical of circus publicity ephemera, and the right-hand panel, with its characteristic composition illustrating the performers of the circus, must have been the sort of influence that affected the work of Chéret.

17 RAMON CASAS
Anís del Mono 1898

18 HENRI DE TOULOUSE-LAUTREC
Jane Avril 1893
Victoria and Albert Museum, London

19 THÉOPHILE-ALEXANDRE STEINLEN
La Traite des Blanches 1899
Other versions of this poster exist, including one in which the bare breasts of the woman on the right

of the design are covered; this followed a ruling by the Préfecture de Police in Paris that the original was indecent.
Stedelijk Museum, Amsterdam

20 LEO PUTZ
Moderne Galerie *c.* 1914

21 CHARLES RENNIE MACKINTOSH
The Scottish Musical Review 1896
Mackintosh (1868–1928) and his associates at the Glasgow School of Art were known as The Four. The others were his wife Margaret Macdonald, Herbert McNair, and McNair's wife, Frances, who was Margaret's sister. The mural designs and architecture produced at Glasgow were even more stylized than the poster illustrated here.
Collection of the Museum of Modern Art, New York. Acquired by exchange

22 KOLOMAN MOSER
Ver Sacrum 1903
V.E.B. Verlag der Kunst, Dresden

23 ALFRED ROLLER
Poster for XIVth Exhibition, Vienna Secession 1902
Albertina, Vienna

24 EMIL PREETORIUS
Poster for an exhibition 1911
Museum für Deutsche Geschichte, Berlin (D.D.R.)

25 OLAF GULBRANSSON
Conrad Dreher 1912
Museum für Deutsche Geschichte, Berlin (D.D.R.)

26 PIERRE BONNARD
La Revue Blanche 1894
The avant-garde review, *La Revue Blanche*, which ran from 1891 until 1903, was founded by the brothers Alexandre and Thadée Natanson. The technique of using flat patterns and texture – as in the boy's scarf in this poster – was developed by Bonnard in many of his paintings at this time. This decorative use of textile materials – in checks, for example – also appears in Jugendstil design and in German poster designs made just before the First World War. An example is Hohlwein's poster *Hermann Scherrer* (ill. 125). The contribution made by Bonnard to the language of poster design comes not only from his few posters but also from his work in general.
Bibliothèque Nationale, Paris. Photo: Giraudon

27 PIERRE BONNARD
France-Champagne 1891
Bibliothèque Nationale, Paris. Photo: Giraudon

28 EUGÈNE GRASSET
Salon des Cent 1894
Victoria and Albert Museum, London

29 ALPHONSE MUCHA
Salon des Cent 1896
Photo: Giraudon

30 MANUEL ORAZI
La Maison Moderne *c.* 1905
Musée des Arts Décoratifs, Paris

31 HECTOR GUIMARD
Exposition Salon du Figaro le Castel Béranger 1900
Collection of the Museum of Modern Art, New York. Gift of Mrs Lillian Nassall

32 EMILE BERCHMANS
Libotte-Thiriar beers *c.* 1897

33 ARPAD BASCH
Poster for Kühnee agricultural machinery

34 EDWARD PENFIELD
Design for Harper's Magazine March, 1894

35 WILL CARQUEVILLE
Lippincott's

36 Posters in a London street 1899
Photo: *Aerofilms Ltd*

37 DUDLEY HARDY
A Gaiety Girl *c.* 1895
Victoria and Albert Museum, London

38 AUBREY BEARDSLEY
Poster for Avenue Theatre, London
1894
In his study of Aubrey Beardsley,
published in 1967, Brian Reade
quotes the following extract from
the poem 'Ars Postera', in Owen
Seaman's *The Battle of the Bays*
(1896):
Mr Aubrey Beer de Beers,
  You're getting quite a high renown;
Your comedy of Leers, you know,
  Is posted all about the town;
This sort of stuff I cannot puff,
  As Boston says, it makes me 'tired';
Your Japanese-Rossetti girl
  Is not a thing to be desired.

Victoria and Albert Museum, London

39 FRED WALKER
The Woman in White 1871
Victoria and Albert Museum, London

40 CARL STRAHTMANN
Music sheet design

41 GEORGES DE FEURE
Le Journal des Ventes 1897

42 FERNAND KHNOPFF
Les XX 1891

43 ANONYMOUS
Mérodak (Salon de la Rose + Croix)
c. 1897
Sotheby and Co

44 FÉLICIEN ROPS
Les Légendes Flamandes 1858
Copyright Bibliothèque royale Albert
1er, Brussels (Cabinet des Estampes)

45 ARMAND POINT AND LÉONARD
SARLUIS
Salon de la Rose + Croix 1896

Collection of Robert Pincus-Witten,
New York City

46 ADOLPHO HOHENSTEIN
Iris 1898

47 MANUEL ORAZI
Loïe Fuller 1900
Many designers made posters of
the American dancer Loïe Fuller,
whose Paris debut took place at
the Folies Bergère in 1893. She
presented an exotic 'light show' in
which she wore long transparent
dresses and veils, creating interpretations of Art Nouveau patterns
such as 'The Serpent Dance'.
Librairie Documents, Paris

48 WILL BRADLEY
The Chap Book 1894

49 JOSEF RUDOLPH WITZEL
Jugend *c.* 1900
This poster was one of those that
were exhibited at the University of
California, Berkeley, in 1965 and
attracted the attention of young
designers; it therefore provides an
interesting link between the bizarre
designs of the 1960s and the posters
of 1900.
Kunsthalle, Bremen

50 BEGGARSTAFF BROTHERS
Girl on a Sofa 1895
The illustration of this poster by
the Beggarstaffs (William Nicholson and James Pryde) was taken
from an issue of *Das Plakat* published in 1914. The publishers of
that magazine chose to print it in
sharp colours that accentuate the
flat pattern in an almost 'abstract'
way. Most of the actual versions of
the original poster have acquired a
mellow colouring, so that if one
were reproduced today it would
give the impression of the traditional elements of the design and

269

not the abbreviated shorthand of the simple pattern. It is also interesting to see that *Das Plakat* recognized the possibilities of this economic composition and its appeal in 1914.

51 JOSEF SATTLER
Pan 1895

52 BOB MASSÉ
Poster for Kitsilano Theatre, Vancouver 1968

ROBERT MCCLAY
Funky Features 1968

54 VICTOR MOSCOSO
Hawaii Pop Rock Festival 1967
Collection of the Museum of Modern Art, New York. Gift of the designer

55 HENRY VAN DE VELDE
Tropon 1897
Stedelijk Museum, Amsterdam

56 PALLADINI
Medusa 1968
This poster was used to advertise Emilio Carballido's production of *Medusa* during the International Festival of Arts held at Jiminez Rueda Theatre, Mexico City, in 1968 for the XIXth Olympic Games.
Victoria and Albert Museum, London

57 LOREN REHBOCK
Peace 1967
By permission of Lorin Gillette, San Francisco

58 PETER MAX
Love 1967
Copyright 1971, Peter Max Enterprises, Inc.

59 BOB SEIDEMANN
Pig Pen, Organist of the Grateful Dead Band 1966

60 VICTOR MOSCOSO
Young Bloods 1967

Distributed by the Print Mint, California

61 T. PRIVAT-LIVEMONT
Cercle Artistique de Schaerbeek 1897
Stedelijk Museum, Amsterdam

62 PAUL CHRISTODOULOU
Elliott: Alice Boots 1967
Dunn-Meynell Keefe Ltd

63 MILTON GLASER
Dylan 1967
Poster designed for Columbia Records by Push Pin Studios Inc.

64 BOB SCHNEPF
Avalon Ballroom 1967

65 BRADBURY THOMPSON
Flower Child 1967

66 JOOST SCHMIDT
Poster for Bauhaus exhibition 1923
Collection of the Museum of Modern Art, New York. Gift of Walter Gropius

67 GISPEN
Rotterdam-South American Line 1927

68 NÖCKUR
Pressa 1928
This poster and its companion piece (ill. 69) have the same theme but treat the subject in contrasting styles.

69 EHMCKE
Pressa 1928

70 WLADIMIR LEBEDEW
Red Army and Navy 1919
V.E.B. Verlag der Kunst, Dresden

71 ROBERT BÉRENY
Poster for Modiano cigarettes

72 WALTER KAMPMANN
Der Spiritismus 1921

73 CASSANDRE
Nicolas 1935
The image of Nectar (and his companion Félicité) was created by Paul Iribe (d. 1935). It was used by Dransy in 1922 (ill. 74) and then, later, by Cassandre in 1935 when the traditional image was given a more progressive background, anticipating later developments in optical painting movements by several decades.
Collection of the Museum of Modern Art, New York

74 DRANSY
Dépôt Nicolas 1922
Victoria and Albert Museum, London

75 CASSANDRE
Étoile du Nord 1927
This poster announced the introduction of a Pullman car service from Paris to Brussels and Amsterdam.
Bibliothèque Nationale, Paris. Photo: Giraudon

76 CASSANDRE
Dubo-Dubon-Dubonnet 1934

77 PIET ZWART
Either 1930
Stedelijk Museum, Amsterdam

78 OTTO BAUMBERGER
Forster 1930

79 JAN TSCHICHOLD
Graphic Design 1927
V.E.B. Verlag der Kunst, Dresden

80 OSKAR SCHLEMMER
Grosse Brücken Revue 1926
Collection of the Museum of Modern Art, New York. Purchase fund

81 BORIS PRUSAKOV
I Hurry to See the Khaz Push 1927
Collection of the Museum of Modern Art, New York

82 EL LISSITZKY
Poster for Russian Exhibition, Zürich 1929
Collection of the Museum of Modern Art, New York. Gift of Philip Johnson

83 G. KLUTSIS
Transport Achievement of the First Five-Year Plan 1929
Collection of the Museum of Modern Art, New York

84 EL LISSITZKY
Beat the Whites with the Red Wedge 1919

85 DZIGA VERTOV
The Man with the Ciné Camera 1928
The poster advertises a film that is concerned with the exploitation of film-editing techniques – of superimposing one image on another – and is accordingly itself a demonstration of these same methods in poster design.

86 EL LISSITZKY
Pelikan Ink 1924
V.E.B. Verlag der Kunst, Dresden

87 LÁSZLÓ MOHOLY-NAGY
Pneumatik 1926
V.E.B. Verlag der Kunst, Dresden

88 LÁSZLÓ MOHOLY-NAGY
Militarismus 1924
Florian Kupferberg Verlag, Mainz

89 LÁSZLÓ MOHOLY-NAGY
Circus and Variety c. 1925
Florian Kupferberg Verlag, Mainz

90 JOSEF MÜLLER-BROCKMAN
Concert poster for Zürich Town Hall 1960

91 THORN PRIKKER
Dutch Exhibition in Krefeld 1903
Stedelijk Museum, Amsterdam

92 Posters on display in Germany 1917

271

the environment. Illustrations also show the design applied to cars and to the interior of buses.

125 LUDWIG HOHLWEIN
Hermann Scherrer 1911
Collection of the Museum of Modern Art, New York. Gift of Peter Muller-Munk

126 LUCIAN BERNHARD
Stiller 1907–08

127 GIOVANNI PINTORI
Olivetti 82 Diaspron
Olivetti Ltd

128 M. DUDOVICH
Olivetti
Olivetti Ltd

129 ANONYMOUS
Imperator (from *Das Plakat*) *c.* 1914

130 PAUL SCHEURICH
Dennerts Lexikon

131 CROSBY/FLETCHER/FORBES
Pirelli 1960s

132 RUDOLPH ALTRICHTER
ATD . . . (A Small Nation also Wants to Live) 1964
By permission of the artist

133 DOLLIERS
The Good Reward *c.* 1916

134 EUGENE MAX CORDIER
German State Railways 1955

135 KARL GERSTNER
Computer programming sheet for Prinzl Bräu *c.* 1968
The programming sheet relates to a large luminous sign 30 metres long by 6 metres high. It is connected up in 92 sections switched in a 30-second cycle. The sign is an extension of the conventional poster, although the sheet itself acts as a brilliant form of design in advertising. It is included here as an example of the highly technical nature of the role of designer at the end of the 1960s.

136 F. H. K. HENRION
Go Super National Benzole 1960

137 EUGENIO CARMI
Safety Sign 1968
An example of one of Carmi's designs in which instructions are presented in a brief, visual sign-language. The element of the sign in relation to posters is given a clear connection in this context.
By permission of the artist

138 MARCELLO NIZZOLI
Olivetti 1950
Olivetti Ltd

139 HERBERT LEUPIN
Poster for a Printer in Lausanne 1959

140 TOM ECKERSLEY
Poster for General Post Office 1952

141 HANS HILLMAN
Kiel Week 1964
By permission of the artist

142 AKIRA UNO
Horror of the Sea of Silence
Japan Cultural Society, Tokyo. Photo: Eileen Tweedy

143 JAN LEWITT AND GEORGE HIM
Post Office Lines of Communication 1950

144 HENDRIK CASSIERS
Red Star Line *c.* 1914

145 JO STEINER
Bier: Cabaret 1919
By permission of Anton Sailer, Karl Thieing, Munich

146 G. M. MATALONI
Bec-Auer Gas Mantles 1895

147 KARPELLUS
Koh-i-Noor

273

148 OSKAR KOKOSCHKA
Poster for the Artists' Union summer exhibition, Dresden 1921
Stedelijk Museum, Amsterdam

149 ERNST LUDWIG KIRCHNER
Die Brücke 1910
Kaiser Wilhelm Museum, Krefeld

150 WASSILY KANDINSKY
Poster for the New Artists' Union exhibition 1909
Museum für Deutsche Geschichte, Berlin (D.D.R.)

151 OSKAR KOKOSCHKA
Der Sturm

152 ÉDOUARD DUYCK AND ADOLPHE CRESPIN
Alcazar Royal – Bruxelles Sans-Gène 1894
This poster was designed for the revue *Bruxelles Sans-Gène*, and is composed of an imaginary audience of well-known personalities and local celebrities.

153 OTTO STAHL-ARPKE
The Cabinet of Dr Caligari 1919
Collection of the Museum of Modern Art, New York. Gift of Universum-Film Aktiengesellschaft

154 ROMAN CIEŚLEWICZ
The Trial 1964

155 JEFIM CWIK
May Day 1965
By permission of the artist

156 H. N. WERKMAN
Poster for a lecture on modern art 1920
Stedelijk Museum, Amsterdam

157 HEMELMAN
Northern Cruises 1926

158 EITAKU KANO
Herbal Pharmacy 1897
Art Directors' Club of Tokyo

159 BURKH-MONGOLD
Federal Swiss Song Festival 1905
Sotheby and Co

160 BART VAN DER LECK
Rotterdam-London 1919
Stedelijk Museum, Amsterdam

161– GAN HOSOYA
62 Posters for Sapporo Breweries 1968
By permission of Bijutsu Shuppan-Sha, Tokyo

163 GEORGE TSCHERNY
Poster for the School of Visual Arts, New York 1961
By permission of the artist

164 J. C. LYENDECKER
Chesterfield Cigarettes 1926
Bruckmann Verlag, Munich

165 ATELIER YVA, BERLIN
Jelsbach & Co *c.* 1927

166 YUSAKA KAMEKURA
Kokudo Keikaku Co. Ltd 1968
By permission of Bijutsu Shuppan-Sha, Tokyo

167 ANONYMOUS
Nelbarden Swimwear 1969

168 KURT SCHWITTERS AND THEO VAN DOESBURG
Poster for Dada recital in The Hague 1923
By permission of Eckhard Neumann

169 SALVADOR DALI
Roussillon (French Railways) 1969

170 TETSUO MIYAHARA
Jazz St Germain 1968
By permission of the artist

171 GRANDVILLE
Metamorphoses 1854
Grandville was the name used by Jean Ignace Isadore Gérard. His designs, which anticipate the frightening anthropomorphisms of Max Ernst, contain many ex-

amples like this illustration, for instance, *La Vie Privée et Publique des Animaux*, which was completed in 1867.

172 FERDINAND LUNEL
Rouxel and Dubois *c.* 1896
Bibliothèque Nationale, Paris

173 TAMANGO
Terrot Cycles and Automobiles 1898

174 CHOUBRAC
Humber Cycles *c.* 1896
Bibliothèque Nationale, Paris

175 SKAWONIUS
Swedish theatre poster *c.* 1938

176 T. MORALIS
Greece 1952

177 GEORGE HIM
The Times 1952

178 HERBERT MATTER
All Roads Lead to Switzerland 1935
Collection of the Museum of Modern Art, New York. Gift of Bernard Davis

179 JEAN D'YLEN
Shell 1924
By permission of The Studio

180 A. CHOUBRAC
Lavabos
Bibliothèque Nationale, Paris

181 JOHN HEARTFIELD (HELMUT HERZ-FELD)
For the Crisis Party Convention of the S.P.D. 1931
Collection of the Museum of Modern Art, New York

182 FRANCIŠZEK STAROWIEYSKI
Brazilian film poster 1969

183 ALAN ALDRIDGE
Film poster for Andy Warhol's Chelsea Girls 1968

Copyright 1970. Published by Motif Editions, London

184 MILTON GLASER (PUSH PIN STUDIOS INC.)
From Poppy with Love 1967
By permission of the artist

185 PETER MAX
Outer Space 1967
Victoria and Albert Museum, London

186 PIETER BRATTINGA
Carnaval 1958
Stedelijk Museum, Amsterdam

187 TEISSIG
Polish poster for French film 1966
Stedelijk Museum, Amsterdam

188 TADANORI YOKOO
Laboratory of Play *c.* 1968
By permission of the artist

189 WALDEMAR SWIERZY
Polish travel poster 1969

190 TADANORI YOKOO
Theatre poster *c.* 1968
By permission of the artist

191 SHIGERU MIWA
Poster advertising a collection of modern American short stories *c.* 1968
By permission of the artist

192 HARRY GORDON
Wonderwall 1969
Cinecenta Ltd

193 JOHN HASSALL
Blackpool *c.* 1912
This unassuming poster by Hassall is clearly related to the snapshot. It provides a contrast to some of the pretentious poster designs using the subject of children that appeared in the nineteenth century. The most famous of these was the painting *Bubbles* by Sir John Millais, which was bought and subsequently used as an advertisement by Pears Soap.

277

246 HIROKATSU HIJIKATA
No More Hiroshimas! 1968
By permission of the artist

247 CUZIN
Set of posters from Michelin
Studios, Paris 1971
The original O'Galup design,
which featured 'Bibendum' (the
fat man made up of tyres), is here
given a dynamic, abstract formula
that suggests speed and perhaps the
movement of the wide cinema
screen – itself a product of the large
billboard. The posters for Michelin
were issued on a large scale –
16 square metres in area – and
when seen in isolation appeared as
gigantic paintings with minimal
reference to the product. The
illustrations reproduced here were
taken from exactly the same designs made on Perspex on a miniature scale for use as display cards
for the Paris Métro.

248 XANTI
Mussolini 1934
The image of the totalitarian state
and its leader is given the same
form as that used in the title-page
of Thomas Hobbes's *Leviathan*
(1651).

249 MANCHE
Nazi recruiting poster used in the
Netherlands, Second World War
Elsevier Nederland N.V., Amsterdam

250 VOSKUIL
Poster for exhibition commemo-
rating the Olympic Games under
Nazi patronage 1936
Stedelijk Museum, Amsterdam

251 HAPSHASH AND THE COLOURED COAT
UFO Mk II 1967
Work produced by this studio was
distributed by Osiris Visions. Its
best known artist, Michael English,

made many highly original posters,
and designed a three-dimensional
shopfront (featuring a car) for a
shop in King's Road, Chelsea,
London.
Victoria and Albert Museum, London

252 HENRI MONTASSIER
La Machine à Finir la Guerre
1917–18
Imperial War Museum, London

253 MIECZSLAW TOMKIEWICZ
To the West! 1945

254 ANONYMOUS
Assassin (anti-American poster
issued in France by the Nazis) 1943
Bibliothèque Nationale, Paris

255 KÄTHE KOLLWITZ
No More War 1924
*Photo: courtesy of Galerie St Etienne,
New York*

256 ATELIER POPULAIRE
La Chienlit c'est lui! 1968
Bibliothèque Nationale, Paris

257 Chinese Communist government
poster
Photo: Camera Press

258 WILLIAM WEEGE
Fuck the CIA! 1967
Courtesy of Art and Artists

259 SEYMOUR CHWAST (PUSH PIN
STUDIOS, INC.)
End Bad Breath 1967
*Poster Prints, Conshohocken, Penn-
sylvania*

260 ANONYMOUS
Long Live the Third Communist
International!
The Third Communist International, or Comintern, was set up
in 1919, and encouraged revolution against capitalist countries for

many years. It was dissolved in 1943.

261 ANONYMOUS
Cuban political poster 1970
Collection of Peter Adam, London

262 RAÚL MARTINÉZ
Painting 1966
Collection of Peter Adam, London

263 ANONYMOUS
WR – The Mysteries of the Organism (poster for Yugoslav film) 1971
By permission of Dilys Powell

264 EMORY DOUGLAS
Trick or Treat (Black Panther poster) 1970

265 V. HUSSAR
Miss Blanche (De Stijl display) 1927

266 FORTUNATO DEPERO
Pavilion 1927

267 HERBERT BAYER
Newspaper kiosk (Bauhaus display) 1924

268 ANONYMOUS
Royal Ediswan lamps. Freak car 1927

269 ANONYMOUS
Electrolux Ltd. Freak car 1927

270–
73 ARTUR GUMITSCH
Three-dimensional displays from the 1930s

Index

Page numbers in italics refer to illustrations

284

286